GOD'S
PLAY
BOOK

Also by Reggie White

In the Trenches: The Autobiography

Reggie White: Minister of Defense

*The Reggie White Touch Football Playbook:
Winning Plays, Rules, and Safety Tips*

Also by Steve Hubbard

*Shark Among Dolphins: Inside Jimmy Johnson's
Transformation of the Miami Dolphins*

*Faith In Sports: Athletes and Their Religion
on and off the Field*

How to Raise an MVP: Most Valuable Person

Today's Heroes: David Robinson

Great Running Backs: Football's Fearless Foot Soldiers

The 1993 Fantasy Football Insider

GOD'S

THE BIBLE'S GAME

PLAY

PLAN FOR LIFE

BOOK

REGGIE WHITE

WITH STEVE HUBBARD

A
JANET
THOMA
BOOK

THOMAS NELSON PUBLISHERS
Nashville

Published in Nashville, Tennessee, by Thomas Nelson, Inc., Publishers

Scripture quotations noted NKJV are from THE NEW KING JAMES VERSION. Copyright © 1979, 1980, 1982, 1990 Thomas Nelson, Inc., Publishers.

Scripture quotations noted NIV are from the HOLY BIBLE: NEW INTERNATIONAL VERSION®. Copyright © 1973, 1978, 1984 by International Bible Society. Used by permission of Zondervan Publishing House. All rights reserved.

Scripture quotations noted KJV are from the KING JAMES VERSION.

Library of Congress Cataloging-in-Publication Data

White, Reggie.
    God's playbook : the Bible's game plan for life / Reggie White with Steve Hubbard.
        p.   cm.
    ISBN 0-7852-8031-6 (hardcover)
    1. Christian life—Baptist authors. 2. White, Reggie. I. Hubbard, Steve (Steve A.)
II. Title.
BV4501.2.W4498   1998
248.4'86—dc21   98-29418
                                                     CIP

Printed in the United States of America
1 2 3 4 5 6 BVG 03 02 01 00 99 98

To my wife,

Sara,

and my children,

Jeremy and Jecolia

CONTENTS

INTRODUCTION
A PLAYBOOK FOR LIFE

I remember my first game of Little League. I was ten years old, playing center field for the Giants. The Pirates had a big kid who threw extremely hard, and I was afraid of getting clobbered by one of his pitches. We got two or three men on base, and I remember standing in the batter's box and asking the Lord, "Please let me hit a home run."

The pitcher zipped his first two pitches by me for strikes. I said, "Forget it. It's not going to happen. God doesn't answer kids' prayers, just adults' prayers." I was scared. The third pitch, I just closed my eyes and swung.

And hit a home run!

I'll never forget it. I sprinted around the bases until I got to third base, where my coach said, "Slow down, son, you hit a home run." Matter of fact, one of my friends ran out to get the ball, and I'd hit it so hard, it screamed over the fence and bull-dozed right into the ground.

Before that day, I had thought God was real, but I didn't figure I was old enough for Him to answer my prayers. Maybe some people will think the home run was coincidence, that God has better things to do than help ten year olds hit home runs, but that home run convinced me God would answer any and everybody's prayers. That answered prayer also made me realize I needed to learn more about who God was.

I was saved at thirteen, made a real commitment at fifteen, and became a licensed minister at seventeen. I became known as the Minister of Defense for the University of Tennessee Volunteers, as an All-Pro defensive end for the Philadelphia Eagles, and as the NFL's all-time sack leader and a Super Bowl champion for the Green Bay Packers. And, I hope most of all, as an ordained minister who fervently believes in God.

The Bible is more than just a book to me. The Bible is my life. It is the basis for everything I do. I like the way Tunch Ilkin put it. Tunch was a Pro Bowl lineman for the Pittsburgh Steelers before finishing his career alongside me with the Packers. Tunch said, "The Steelers had a playbook with 150 plays. If we mastered them, we could win. God has a playbook too. It's called the Bible. Everything we need to know is in God's playbook."

The football analogy is a good one. The Bible is our playbook for life. Its game plan details how we can live a rich, rewarding life. It offers answers to questions about family and faith and career fulfillment, in times of trouble or triumph. This playbook reshapes our lives, if we let it.

It's an instructional book that shows how flawed men turned their lives around and became righteous men, men who benefited society. A lot of times people think those biblical people were perfect, but if we really read the Bible, we'll see they were not. Guys like Moses and David and Paul were murderers. There were tax collectors, like Matthew, who were thieves. God turned a bunch of bad people into good people.

The stories might be thousands of years old, but the wisdom is just as relevant in the new millennium as it ever was. I apply the Bible's ancient principles to my life every day. It's fun. I see what God did for these men and women, and I begin to understand, "Hey, even though I was a bad person, God can change me if I give Him a chance." That's why I enjoy reading God's Word; He challenges me to change.

I've read self-help books on faith, on marriage, on business, on specific issues I've dealt with, and some have spoken to me and helped me. But to be honest with you, I don't read too many books, because I keep going back to the best self-help book of all time. And the Bible is more than self-help. The Bible is a book that can give you a life-changing experience. There is a reason it is the best-selling and most inspiring book in the world: it works!

I know that most people would not listen to me if I was not a football player. I realize God has given me this position for a reason. Not to be made into an idol, but to be used to present His Word and His message to the world and to become their hero. I want to use my fame to impact people's lives. So the most important thing in my life is to share the message, not in a pushy way, but to let you see, "Hey, this guy is real. He can identify with me." I know people sometimes think pro athletes are untouchable, but believe me, we struggle with many of the same issues you do.

The goal of *God's Playbook* is to share some of the lessons I've learned from the Bible, from football, and from life, from all my coaches, teachers, mentors, and ministers, in hopes these lessons will help you too. This book is not an autobiography. This is a devotional guide for you, the reader. It's broken into twelve books of essays.

I've taken lessons from the Bible, from my life and career, and arranged them in a dozen topics about enhancing our lives:

- The Book of Goals discusses setting and reaching your goals.
- The Book of Miracles details how you can become a winner and achieve miracles in your life.

- The Book of Knowledge goes beyond book learning to focus on using role models and mentors to improve ourselves.

- The Book of Focus talks about concentrating on our goals, not fears or distractions, in order to reach the mountaintop.

- The Book of Work focuses on finding the balance between hard work and a good life.

- The Book of Teamwork imparts some lessons that made the Green Bay Packers into Super Bowl champions.

- The Book of Communication explores ways to improve how we talk and listen to others.

- The Book of Character deals with problems and issues we all face.

- The Book of Obstacles focuses on hurdling the inevitable walls we run into.

- The Book of Faith emphasizes faith in God and self.

- The Book of Love centers on what I've learned about building better relationships.

- The Book of Fulfillment shares lessons about leading a richer, more rewarding life.

I want to make the Bible come alive. I want to show how it applies to life in the twentieth and twenty-first centuries. Because we can't do things the way we did twenty or thirty years ago. We've got a new and different generation and a lot of people who don't like church. Hey, let's face it: Some churches are boring. Some are dynamite. Those dynamite churches have figured out ways to relate to people, and that's what I'm trying to do too.

You don't have to be a faithful churchgoer to get something out of this book. If you've been turned off by church, if you think the Bible is just a bunch of myths about dead guys who have nothing in common with you, I encourage you to pick up this book and explore with me. I'm not putting pressure on people, not pounding them upside the head the way I do offensive linemen and quarterbacks come Sunday in the fall. But I hope people who read this book will decide, "It *does* make sense. He deals with the same everyday issues I deal with."

I hope to show you some answers, and I hope you will decide to go to the Word and learn more. I hope you will realize just how motivational the Bible is, and see how you can develop a spiritual connection and improve your life.

Because I know that without my faith—and without what I have learned from it—I would have achieved nothing in football and in life.

PART ONE

THE BOOK
OF GOALS

BEGIN WITH VISION

Your young men shall see visions,
Your old men shall dream dreams.
Acts 2:17

When I was twelve years old, I told my mother I would become a pro football player and a minister.

"A minister?" she said, incredulous. She believed I could be a pro football player, but she didn't understand the minister part.

But I knew there was a purpose for what I was doing, and I was confident that I could achieve the vision God had instilled in me. He had given me an ability, and I was not going to waste the opportunity.

Sure, both visions seemed far-fetched at the time. For every million boys who dream of playing pro football, maybe one winds up an All-Pro. And when I was twelve, I wasn't even playing football. I was playing baseball, and my goal was to break Hank Aaron's home run record. But then I watched an NFL Films highlight reel on O.J. Simpson, and I got fired up about tackling him one day. So I started playing football at thirteen, when I went into seventh grade.

Becoming a minister seemed even more unlikely. I had gone to church quite often during the year I lived with my grandmother, after my mother married my stepfather and joined him at his army base in Kansas. But my mother came home to Chattanooga, Tennessee, about the time I turned ten, and for the next few years I went to church sparingly. I was not a bad kid, but I was mischievous. I did everything I could not only to get my way but to get attention.

There weren't many men in my life. My mother and father had never married. He moved from town to town playing professional softball, so he wasn't around a lot. I didn't get along very well with my stepfather. Not understanding what it was to have a father, I really didn't understand what God was about. I could not relate to God as a Father.

I wanted to live right, but I didn't know how. Sometimes I would go to my grandmother's church and listen to Reverend Ferguson, a white pastor at an all-black church. Sometimes I would go to a church in my neighborhood with students from Tennessee Temple. One of them, Ed Christy, became a godly friend, which I needed. He inspired me. I decided I would give my life to the Lord when I was thirteen.

But I was still a kid and confused. I didn't understand a whole lot about religion because I wasn't being discipled. Other than Ed, I didn't really know anyone who could impart what I needed to know to serve God. I remember going to a church function once, and I told a guy I had given my life to Christ and been baptized. He told me I should do it again. I didn't understand why I had to do it again, but I did. I thought every time you sinned, you needed to pray and receive Christ again.

Somebody asked me if I had received Christ and I said, "Yeah, two times." A girl about my age told me I could only be saved once. She said you don't have to ask Him over and over. Finally, I realized, I can ask one time and Jesus will come into my life if I just change my heart.

Football and ministry. I had visions and dreams, and I chased them with all my heart.

DARE TO BE GREAT

With men this is impossible,
but with God all things are possible.
Matthew 19:26 NKJV

I am six feet five inches tall and weigh three hundred pounds. I can bench-press one linebacker in my right hand and another in my left. I have knocked 330-pound offensive linemen onto their behinds and into the hospital. I have left running backs and quarterbacks with concussions and broken bones, and I wasn't even trying to hurt them.

So if we were fighting to the death, what do you think I'd do to a normal man, let alone some scrawny, zit-popping teenager?

If you read 1 Samuel 17, you'll see what I mean. Goliath was a whole lot bigger and nastier than me, and David was just a boy, believed to be between the ages of thirteen and seventeen. Goliath was over nine feet tall, wore a bronze helmet and a coat of armor, and carried a huge sword and spear. I talked about them today when I spoke to the fourth-grade class of my daughter, Jecolia.

Every day for forty days, Goliath had come to the battle line and challenged the men of Israel to fight him. Nobody dared. All the men under Saul, Israel's first king, were terrified of the Philistine giant—until David arrived and vowed to fight.

Saul told him no, that he was just a boy, but David said the God who had saved him from lions and bears would save him from Goliath. Saul tried to fit him in armor, but David found it uncomfortable and discarded it all. The same is true in football and life today: You can't wear someone else's jockstrap. You can't be someone you're not.

So David marched out to face Goliath with only his faith in God, his slingshot, and five smooth stones.

Goliath took one look at David and laughed at him. "You mean to tell me you're sending a boy with rocks and sticks in his hands?" Goliath roared. "I'm going to feed your body to the birds of the air and the beasts of the field."

See, the NBA didn't invent trash talking. Goliath did. But David wasn't intimidated. No, he talked a little trash of his own.

"You really think you're going to come at me with a sword and spear and javelin?" David asked. "I come against you in the name of the Lord God of Israel. Today, I will cut your head off. And this day I will give the carcasses of the whole Philistine army to the birds of the air and wild beasts of the field—and the whole world will know there is a God in Israel."

David ran toward Goliath, killed him with one throw of that slingshot, and cut his head off. The Philistine army ran home, and the Israeli army went after them and killed them. David's prophecy came true: their bodies were fed to the birds of the air and the wild beasts of the field.

This young boy was not afraid of the giant. Why? Because David had a covenant relationship with God. The covenant extended not only to David but to the whole nation of Israel—if only one man would step forward in obedience. David also knew there would be a reward for his obedience. The soldiers told David before he went out to fight Goliath, "Whoever kills this man, the king will give him riches, his daughter, and eliminate his taxes."

It's funny to me that David, just a kid, asked the question again: What would the man get? He was interested in the reward and maybe even the king's daughter. And *everyone* is interested in having his taxes eliminated.

David showed it makes no difference what age we are, God always has a call for us. So dream big dreams. Be bold and courageous. Dare to be great. David did. Because with God, all things are possible.

LET NO ONE DETER YOU FROM YOUR GOALS

I can do all things through Christ
who strengthens me.
Philippians 4:13 NKJV

From the start of middle school to the end of high school, I carried my Bible virtually everywhere I went. I took it to school every day, even though the other kids threw spitballs at me and mocked me. Knowing I'd get laughed at and tested, I kept on carrying it—because I felt God wanted me to take my Bible to school.

All the things I feared most happened. Back then, if you read the Bible or didn't smoke marijuana, they called you a square. I was The Big Square. The Doofus. They called me Goofy—and, I have to admit, I *was* rather goofy when I was young.

They were trying to make me mad to see if I would retaliate. Most of the time I wouldn't, but sometimes I hit kids. See, I was carrying and reading the Bible, but I didn't understand it. Shucks, I remember one time, I had read a Scripture in Psalms where it talked about killing people for lying. I misinterpreted it, and I went around telling kids, "If you don't stop lying, I'll have to kill you."

Our fights never turned nasty. I'd hit a kid in the arm or leg or something like that. My hits hurt, but I wasn't trying to injure anybody. It was almost like they expected me to hit them after they mocked me, and we would laugh it off.

The harassment faded when I got to high school. After all the mess I took from my classmates for three years in middle school, they just expected me to carry the Bible by that time. If I didn't have it with me, they'd say, "What's wrong with you, Reggie?" When you persevere for a long time, people respect you. They test you just to see, "Is this guy for real, or is he doing this just to do this?"

Plus, kids started to respect me because I was such a good athlete. My high school coach, Robert Pulliam, met with the seniors on the football team and told them I was going to be great.

"I asked them to watch out for him," Coach Pulliam remembers. "I knew kids would pick on him for carrying a Bible. I told the captains to make other kids think they were interested in the Bible. The most amazing thing was, a lot of kids grew close to Reggie and the Bible."

Hey, even Noah was mocked. His neighbors laughed at him when he built the ark, and you know who turned out right there, don't you? So when I set my goals of becoming a pro football player and a minister, I was not going to let any silly taunts bother me. Once you have a vision, a direction, a mission in life, you've got to work toward it with a passion. You can't let the doubters dissuade you or you'll achieve nothing in life.

It's funny. As children, we approach life with wonder, as if all dreams are possible. But as we get older and supposedly smarter, we start doubting ourselves and let others convince us we cannot accomplish our goals. We become so afraid of failure, sometimes we don't even try. But why should we have such self-defeating attitudes?

So despite the jokes, I read the Bible every day, and the more I read, the more fascinated I became. When I was just seventeen,

I gave a trial sermon on forgiveness and earned my minister's license. I still had a lot to learn, but I kept working toward my goal.

And I started working to become a better football player. Before I started ninth grade, a buddy who lived down the street said we should start jogging to get in better shape for football practice that fall. We jogged 1.6 miles through the hills at the base of Lookout Mountain, and we made jogging part of our daily routine. We jogged together throughout high school and even when I was home from college, and the hills and distance helped my endurance. That's where my motivation and success began—when I was fourteen years old and Billy Harper told me, "Let's go run."

See, I wasn't blessed with an incredible body. I was tall, but I wasn't big and strong before I started working out. I realized that if I wanted to achieve my goal of becoming a professional football player, I had to work.

I want to be great at what I do, whether it's as a football player or as a man. If I want to be great, I have to work. If I want my team to be great, I have to inspire my teammates to work. Let's face it, most people don't want to work to be great. Because work is hard, not fun. I've seen guys who played off raw ability, working hard during the season, but not during the offseason. But the really great ones work hard all year and build a legacy for generations.

That's what I desire for myself. That's what I desire to implant in my children and my wife and others. You have a real impact when you create other great people.

PART TWO

THE BOOK OF MIRACLES

DEVELOP A
WINNING ATTITUDE

> If you have faith as a mustard seed, you will say
> to this mountain, "Move from here to there,"
> and it will move; and nothing will be impossible for you.
> *Matthew 17:20 NKJV*

When I joined the Packers in 1993, they had not advanced to the NFC or NFL championship game since 1968, back in the Vince Lombardi dynasty days. The team had made the playoffs just twice in twenty-five years. They had improved from 4–12 to 9–7 in Mike Holmgren's first year as coach, but they still didn't make the playoffs, and I sensed a losing mentality pervading Green Bay. It's like Lombardi said: "Winning is a habit. Unfortunately, so is losing."

We won my first game as a Packer, but then we lost three in a row, and I called a meeting.

"I've noticed a problem on this team," I told my new teammates. "A few guys make an excuse for every mistake they make. Other guys are just happy to be here. Some of you guys walk in here when we lose and it doesn't even bother you. I assure you, if I keep seeing that, I will help get you out of here, because I want to win. And the only way we're gonna win is if we get everybody on the same page.

"Let me tell you something: It bothers me to lose. It bothers me big time. I didn't come to Green Bay to lose, and I hope none of you guys did either. From this day on, I hope every man on this team has a grudge against losing. I hope losing puts a knot in your throat and makes you want to put your fist through a wall. Because if losing makes you mad, then you're going to go out there and bust your gut to keep from losing."

We started making some changes and turned the losing habit into a winning habit. We were a playoff team my first two years, but we weren't a championship team, and there's a big difference. We learned the difference in the 1995 season, when we went to San Francisco to play our second-round game. The 49ers were the defending champions, winners of five Super Bowls in fourteen years, and as dominating as ever.

The bookies listed us as ten-point underdogs, and to be honest, we really didn't know if we could win. When the media asked Coach Mike Holmgren if we could win the Super Bowl, he said yes. Some of the 49ers used that as a motivational ploy, and we were surprised the Super Bowl champions needed something like that to inspire them. It didn't make sense to us, because what else is a coach to say? "No, we can't win"? So we decided the 49ers were somewhat intimidated.

Maybe our smash-for-cash program gave us an incentive too. When I was in Philly, we used to get a hundred dollars for every big play—a sack, interception, forced fumble, fumble recovery, touchdown, or big hit. Even guys making millions seemed more excited about that hundred dollars than picking up five-figure game checks. So we ran a similar program in Green Bay. When the fund ran out of money near the end of the year, Sean Jones and I kicked in some extra cash to keep it going. I was trying to motivate my guys because I was the defensive leader.

The very first play on defense, Wayne Simmons belted 49ers running back Adam Walker, forced a fumble, and Craig Newsome picked up the ball and ran it in for a touchdown. That gave us the confidence we could beat them, and our confidence just built more and more, because the next two times our offense got the ball, Brett Favre threw touchdowns. We were ahead 21–0 by early in the second quarter. We played our best game as a team all year, and we won, 27–17.

I was paying five hundred dollars for each big play. I don't know if it was the motivating factor for the upset, but you should have seen how excited the guys were when I doled out the dough during a team meeting that week. That first play cost me $1,500—five hundred each for the forced fumble, recovered fumble, and touchdown. Guys made so many sacks and interceptions and big hits, I paid out $9,000 of my $13,000 game check. If I had done it for the whole team and not just the defense, the victory would have cost me my entire check.

But it was worth it, because that was the most memorable upset in my career and the turning point in the way we viewed ourselves. I think that win set up our Super Bowl victory the following year. Upsetting the 49ers gave us confidence we could beat an elite team. And you must convince yourself that you *can* win the big game, that you *can* overcome seemingly insurmountable obstacles, even when other people doubt you, even when you have reason to doubt yourself.

It takes more than just belief, though. Plenty of times I've known in my heart we were going to win, but we didn't. You also need talent, effort, camaraderie, and determination. When you get tired of losing and you look at winning as the only thing, as Vince Lombardi said, then you'll start winning.

Winners always have new goals to reach. If they win one title, they think, "Now I want to be part of a dynasty." When we won Super Bowl XXXI, I didn't detect a lot of arrogance or inflated egos. We went back to the Super Bowl but fell short, and I'm like Lombardi: I don't like second place. I want to win one more Super Bowl before I retire. I want to move mountains.

WINNING IT ALL

This Book of the Law shall not depart from your mouth,
but you shall meditate in it day and night, that you may
observe to do according to all that is written in it.
For then you will make your way prosperous,
and then you will have good success.

Joshua 1:8 NKJV

As high as I felt when we upset San Francisco, that's how low
I felt after we lost the NFC championship game in Dallas. Not
only was I tormented by the loss, I was furious with referee Ed
Hochuli. Cowboys right tackle Erik Williams stuck his fingers
through my face mask and scratched me until I started bleed-
ing. That's a face-mask penalty, but Hochuli missed it.

Then Erik started clobbering my helmet. If you've ever put
on a helmet and gotten a head slap, you know how much that
hurts and why the NFL outlawed it decades ago. Erik punched
me in the face, and that's illegal too. But every time I told the referee, he wouldn't call it or even say anything to Erik. And finally
he told me I needed to quit whining and just play football. That's
an insult to my integrity and my profession, because I don't say
things just to say them. We were also furious when Erik chopped
defensive tackle John Jurkovic so savagely that it bruised Jurko's
knee. It might have been a legal hit, but it wasn't moral.

I was too mad to cry, but many a grown man shed tears in our locker room. One player kicked a trash can and sent it flying like a field goal attempt. Another knocked over a cooler full of ice and Gatorade.

On the bus ride to the airport, Brett Favre told me, "Big Dog, I promise you, we're gonna win it all next year."

And I made the same promise to him.

The Dallas defeat motivated us, but beating San Francisco is what took us to the next level in confidence. When we went to training camp in 1996, Brett proclaimed, "Super Bowl or bust," and LeRoy Butler bragged, "We're the team to beat now." And we were.

We won the NFC championship that year against Carolina, and I took a victory lap around the field, high-fiving as many Lambeau Field fans as I could. Brett ran over and hugged me and shouted in my ear, "Reggie, this is why you came to Green Bay! This is your moment! You deserve this!"

I had won eleven consecutive Pro Bowl berths, an NFL Defensive Player of the Year award, a Pro Bowl MVP trophy, and the NFL sack record. But I was thirty-five years old and had never won a championship of any kind. Not in high school, college, or the pros. Not in football, checkers, or pie eating. I had begun to fear that my championship quest was futile.

But we went to New Orleans, and I finally fulfilled my fantasy when we beat the New England Patriots in Super Bowl XXXI.

I'd like to say I savored every delicious moment of that 35–21 victory and my record-setting three sacks, but honestly, I was so exhausted, I can't remember a whole lot about the celebration. I do recall standing up on the podium for the presentation of the Vince Lombardi Trophy. When they handed me the microphone on live, worldwide TV, I made sure to thank God in front of hundreds of millions of viewers.

That was important to me, because when I left Philadelphia in 1993, I said I would go where the Lord sent me and where I could win a championship. A lot of the media criticized me for choosing Green Bay. They said God didn't care where I played football and I certainly wouldn't win a Super Bowl in Green Bay. Some said I only went there because the Packers offered the most money.

I'm not going to lie to you, money played a factor. But I also felt Green Bay had a quarterback who could take this team to the championship, and Green Bay made a four-year commitment to me when San Francisco, my other top choice, was only offering three years. So when I stood on that podium, I wanted to thank God because I knew He was letting the world know, "Hey, I did send him to Green Bay. I blessed him because he listened to Me. I told him what to do and he did it, and blessings will come through obedience."

Then I ran a victory lap around the Superdome, holding the Super Bowl trophy high overhead. I wanted the Green Bay fans to know this trophy was just as much theirs as ours. Through all the terrible years, they had sold out Lambeau Field, sitting out in the cold weather and supporting their team.

With my son, Jeremy, by my side in the locker room, I told reporters, "Now I can sit back with my son for years and watch highlights of this Super Bowl, and he can see Daddy getting three sacks. I thank God for sending me here to Green Bay. Some of you guys thought I was crazy four years ago. But now I'm getting a ring. How crazy do you think I am now?"

PRAY FOR GUIDANCE

Call to Me, and I will answer you,
and show you great and mighty things,
which you do not know.
Jeremiah 33:3 NKJV

I don't follow a set schedule, but I pray often. God talks to me, and I talk to Him. I sought God's advice on whether I should retire or return to the Packers in 1998, but because my back ached so much, I had pretty much made up my mind I was not going to play anymore.

For the last three years, I had contemplated retiring. Sometimes I got tired of the game, and I had a zeal to get on with the ministry full-time, thinking I was slowing down God's calling to play His game. But I know God kept me in the game because there's a purpose to His plan. This game has built my character. It's helped me spiritually. It's helped me as a father and a husband.

But in 1998 I figured it was time to move on. From Super Bowl XXXII in late January to the NFL draft in mid-April, I prayed about it off and on, yet I really didn't hear anything from God. I just knew I was going to retire. I figured that since I had made up my mind, God must have been telling me I wasn't going to play. And when the pain did not let up during the off-season, I took it as one more sign that God wanted me to retire.

Eventually I realized God did not want me to retire. It took a while; I had to endure some adversity before God spoke to me. In March, when I was lambasted after my remarks about gays, abortion, and minorities, I sought God to see exactly what He wanted me to do. That incident made me really get close to the Lord and depend upon Him, and it defined the direction He wanted me to follow.

That direction included one more year of football. It was my best spin move, my best change of direction yet. After we lost the Super Bowl, I had told some of my teammates and my coach that I was retiring. Mike Holmgren warned me to wait until the game's emotions wore off, but the only times I wavered even a little came when I would see the guys, and that never lasted for long. A couple of weeks before the draft, I told Mike I was quitting. He tried to talk me out of it, suggested I could still help the team a lot even as a part-time player, but I was sure.

The second day of the draft, Sunday, April 19, I rode over to the stadium and some guys said Mike wanted to see me. We talked a little bit and he asked me if I had changed my mind. I said no.

He said, "Well, I've got to let the media know. Should I tell them?"

I said, "Sure, you can go ahead and do that."

But once I saw him on television that night, I thought, "Something is not right about this." I wasn't mad at Mike, as some people have portrayed it, because I had given him permission to make the announcement. But when I watched it, I thought, "I should be the one announcing my retirement instead of waiting until the press conference on Wednesday to do it."

The next day I talked to Mike again and also had a conversation with our general manager, Ron Wolf. Then I went to get a massage—and that's when the Lord spoke to me. The room was totally silent, and I was just lying there, getting my back worked on, when the Lord told me I had to fulfill my promise.

When I had signed a five-year extension with the Packers in December 1996, I had promised I would play at least two more years—1997 and 1998. The Lord said, "You're breaking a promise if you retire. You have to be a man of your word and fulfill your promise. You want to retire because you don't want to work to get your back well. I want you to fulfill your commitment."

After months of believing I was totally out of football, within a minute I was totally excited about going back to play. I was not only excited, I felt extreme peace about it.

People ask me, "How can you be sure?"

I always know God has spoken when I feel extreme peace. Before, I wasn't excited about playing. Now I am. I know it's God.

A lot of times people think you're crazy when you say God spoke to you. I didn't hear an audible voice. Nobody came and knocked on the door and said, "Reggie, you should do this." I just heard something in my mind that gave me extreme peace.

I know what that something was. It was the voice of God. Besides, my wife confirmed the decision because God had spoken to her prior to the draft.

REPLACE WORRY WITH
PRAYER AND PREPARATION

> Be anxious for nothing, but in everything by prayer and
> supplication, with thanksgiving, let your requests be made
> known to God; and the peace of God, which surpasses
> all understanding, will guard your hearts and
> minds through Christ Jesus.
> *Philippians 4:6–7 NKJV*

The Jerky Boys have a compact disk on which they imperson-
ate different people when they make phone calls. One guy acted
like an Egyptian musician invited to do a party.

One day I called home and tried to do the same thing. Now,
I've been doing impersonations since I was a kid, and people
think I'm pretty good at them. I've imitated everyone from Elvis
Presley to John Wayne to Muhammad Ali to Rodney
Dangerfield to "Macho Man" Randy Savage to Bill Cosby, every-
thing from the Incredible Hulk to a kennel of different dogs.

So when my son, Jeremy, answered the phone, I launched
into my best Middle Eastern voice.

"Hi, Jeremy, this is the Egyptian musician," I began.

Before I got anything else out of my mouth, he said, "Hi,
Dad."

Just as a kid knows his dad's voice, just as the sheep know
their shepherd's voice (John 10), we will know our Father's

voice if we seek God. Prayer is communicating with the Father. Prayer can be used to confess sin, seek guidance, express desires, and intercede for others. But most important, prayer should be used to build a relationship with God and to come to know His voice.

I prayed for several years before I heard the voice of God, but I've heard it many times since, particularly in the past five years. God brought me to Green Bay, a city where you pretty much have to sit down and listen, because there's nothing else to do. (I'm just joking, Green Bay. You know I love you.)

When God speaks to me, I don't hear an audible voice, although sometimes in my head God's voice sounds like my voice. I'm not saying I'm God or anything. Don't think that for a second. God's voice is just a thought that comes into my mind, and when it does, I realize I couldn't have figured out that thought by myself. Because it's not like I am contemplating or studying; it just comes to my mind so quickly. And when it comes, plenty of times I have said, "Oh, man! God's answer is so simple, why didn't I think of this a long time ago?"

God wants us to communicate with Him because He has a great plan for our lives. For us to fulfill that plan, we have to hear what He's saying and what He's calling us to do. Psalm 46:10 says, "Be still, and know that I am God" (NKJV). Prayer sometimes consists of sitting down and just being quiet and listening.

You know how people say, "Don't just stand there, do something"? I believe God is telling us, "Don't just do something, stand there." God wants us to be quiet sometimes and just meditate. We have to listen before we can learn and obey.

When I stopped talking and started listening to God, He told me I was using my back as an excuse. I was waiting on Him to heal it with another miracle, as He had done with my injuries before. But then I realized we can't just sit back and wait on God to do everything. The other times I was healed, I had worked to help my injuries heal. Most of the people healed by Jesus sought Him out. They made an effort to find the Messiah to be healed.

I had done hardly anything for my back since the Super Bowl. I had ridden the exercise bike probably six or seven times, and that was it. I had gone to a couple of specialists for advice and was encouraged to rest, but it seemed the more I rested, the worse my back got. I figured since I was going to retire, let me keep resting it for a while and see if it gets better. I just wasn't motivated, and that's not like me. But back spasms are much different from the other injuries I'd had. I had never experienced pain like that before, and it just took the motivation out of me. Also, a lot of my strength comes from my back, and without it, I was frustrated.

When I announced I was coming back just two days after Mike Holmgren said I had retired, the media wondered if I would set aside my many offseason appearances and work hard enough to rehabilitate my back. Those writers don't know my heart and my will. They don't know my schedule; it isn't as full as they're speculating. This is my job; I'll make the time. Since I've decided to play again, I've worked my behind off, and I'm going to continue to work my behind off.

I am committing heart and soul, same as always. I've put God on the spot. I've put myself on the spot. I'm not going to sit back and do nothing. People are waiting for me to fall. If I sit back and do nothing, then I embarrass God, I embarrass myself, and I embarrass the people who believe in me.

When I contemplated retirement, I didn't worry about it, because worry is wasted energy. Worry is like a rocking chair: it gives you something to do, but doesn't get you anywhere. All worry does is cause heartache. Better to deal with your problems in a productive, not a destructive, way. So I prayed, I listened, I obeyed, I prepared. Because prayer and preparation precede miracles, and I want another miracle.

DO YOU BELIEVE
IN MIRACLES?

And when Jesus went out He saw a great multitude;
and He was moved with compassion for them,
and healed their sick.
Matthew 14:14 NKJV

Every exam confirmed our worst fears: my hamstring was torn, torn so badly that only surgery would repair it.

Twelve days before Christmas 1995, the Packers announced my season was over, and I cried and limped home. But that night, while chasing my children around the house, I realized my hamstring felt surprisingly good. I headed to the training facility with the Packers' strength and conditioning coach, Kent Johnston, and we put my left leg through strength-testing exercises—and were astonished to see how much stronger it was.

We drove directly to Mike Holmgren's house. Coach was just turning out his Christmas lights and heading to bed when we rang his doorbell. "I thought it was Santa," he said.

That night Santa gave him a three-hundred-pound present. The next day I practiced, and three days later I played. Played well enough to help us reach the National Football Conference championship game.

"Mind-boggling," Mike said. "Reggie's so inspirational. He's like Lazarus. He always comes back and rises from the dead."

Jesus raised Lazarus from the dead. God healed my hamstring. I know it's nothing but a miracle from God, because I wasn't supposed to be walking, let alone running around.

I know some people doubted it was God, even questioned if my hamstring was really torn. To claim my doctor misdiagnosed the injury is an insult and an error. All you have to do is look at the hamstring and you'll know it's torn. I have a hole in my leg where the hamstring is supposed to be attached. You can put your hand on it and feel that it's bundled up in the back of my thigh. The hamstring provides the leg power I need to play, and without surgery to reattach it, I was supposed to lose all that strength.

But I never had the surgery, and I didn't lose all my strength. How can that be? It shouldn't be, to be honest with you. But that's God.

That was one of three miraculous healings I received in less than fourteen months. I tore ligaments and muscles in my left elbow in November 1994, and the doctors thought I'd be out at least two or three weeks, maybe the rest of the year. That would break my streak of consecutive games played at 148. Instead, I came back in three days.

A year later I sprained the medial collateral ligament in my left knee, but again, I played the very next game. Reporters dubbed me "The Miracle Man." One columnist said I went through miracles the way everyone else went through aspirins, that God is my HMO. Funny line, but let me ask: Who would you prefer to heal you? God or an HMO doctor? Jesus is the real Miracle Man.

I could go into a lot more detail about these miracles, about how bad the injuries were, about the many people who said they prayed for me, but I won't, because I discussed them in my autobiography, *In the Trenches,* and I don't want to repeat myself for those of you who read it. I mention them here to help explain the miracles that have occurred since. Miracles far greater than mine.

Here's the exciting part: experiencing not only physical but spiritual healings made me realize that when God grants you a miracle, you need to extend that miracle to others. God has a unique way of doing ministry. As people all over the nation learned about my miracles, lives were touched. The miracles convinced some people that God was real, that He could heal, and I was able to lead some people to the Lord because of it.

I'll give you two examples. One lady asked me to pray for her son who had cancer. So I called the lady and prayed with her concerning her son, but I also prayed with her concerning her own life, and she decided to trust Jesus for her salvation.

Another lady who owned a health-food restaurant was mad at God and mad at me when I announced I was done for the 1995 season. She questioned why God had healed me before and not this time, so she dismissed the idea that God could do anything. The next day I came back and said God had done a miracle, and it blew her mind. That made her realize that God is real, and she called me and said it was almost like God was talking directly to her. We prayed over the phone, and she gave her life to Jesus too.

God gave me a gift. He is calling me to a ministry of healing. That's why we did a healing service in Green Bay. About two thousand people came that day to get prayed for and to get deliverance.

People with alcoholism. People with marital problems. People with all kinds of problems. One lady asked her husband to come. He had cancer and was supposed to live for just six months. He went to the Mayo Clinic the week after we prayed for him, and they opened him up and didn't find any cancer!

We prayed for another lady with cataracts. When she went to the doctor the next day for surgery, she asked the doctor to check her eyes first. He kept asking her why. She said she believed God had healed her. He checked her eyes and she didn't have cataracts at all!

A lot of people were healed in Green Bay. And in San Jose

one lady was healed of AIDS. I don't even know all the stories because I don't want to be tempted to think, "Hey, look at what I did." I want people to realize that God does the healing. It has nothing to do with Reggie White. It's God who does the miracle. I'm just being obedient and extending the miracle. I don't want to do healings on TV, and I don't even like seeing them there, because I fear people will credit the faith healer and not God. TV is important to get out the word of God, but I want to showcase God, not myself.

I don't need to put on a show for anybody or prove anything to anybody. I don't need to add to my credentials. I just want God to do His work and get me out of the way.

NEVER WAVER IN YOUR FAITH
IN GOD'S HEALING POWER

So Jesus had compassion and touched their eyes.
And immediately their eyes received sight,
and they followed Him.
Matthew 20:34 NKJV

Robert Brooks was a terrific receiver for us in 1995. He set
team records for receiving yards and 100-yard games. He
caught 102 passes and scored thirteen touchdowns. But in
October 1996 he tore the patellar tendon, anterior cruciate ligament, and medial collateral ligament in his right knee. Add in
a big bone chip, and the medical experts figured his career was
in serious jeopardy.

Our trainer, Pepper Burruss, said he'd seen people come
back from ACLs and patellar tendons before, but never the two
together. He said if Robert could come back, "it would be the
greatest recovery I've seen in my twenty years as a trainer."

Robert came to me two weeks after the surgery and said,
"Reggie, God told me to ask you to pray for me and He would
heal me. He said after you prayed for me, I'd be able to throw
the crutches down and walk."

We went into the trainer's office. I got some oil and put my
hand on his knee—the laying on of hands—and prayed for
him.

It was a simple prayer, not long. One thing I've learned about prayer is if you look at what the apostles wrote, the prayers weren't complicated when people were healed.

So all I said was, "In Jesus' name, you're healed. You can walk without crutches. I ask for God's power to come into your life."

The doctor had told Robert he would need crutches for six weeks. When he gave Robert a checkup, he was a little shocked to see him walking after only two weeks.

Robert told the doctor, "God has healed me and I don't need these crutches." The doctor checked his knee. Robert was right!

They still didn't think he would be ready to start the 1997 season, but he came back strong, catching sixty passes for more than a thousand yards, leading us back to the Super Bowl, playing well and serving God.

Now Robert Brooks's life is totally changed. He was a good guy before, but the guys who hang out with him have told me that to see him now compared to the way he was is a testimony to God.

A physical healing is great, but a life change is even better. Physical healings don't last; people eventually die. But a spiritual healing is forever and ever.

I have seen many teammates and NFL peers transformed spiritually. To see where Keith Jackson is now compared to where he was before he found God, you would be totally impressed with the way he has changed his life.

God has also changed the life of Fred Barnett, whom I played with in Philadelphia. We had a young kid in Philadelphia named Mike Flores who joked about my walk with the Lord and wanted guys to laugh at me, but now God has changed his life. A young player who lived with me when I was in Philadelphia, Cedrick Brown, pastors a church now.

I don't think I had an influence, but when Irving Fryar committed his life to the Lord, he called me. He and his wife made a huge change. Cris Carter committed his life to the Lord in Philly, but he went back to his old ways until he recommitted to God about five years ago. He's going all out now. Cris and Irving have joined me as ordained ministers, and Irving is working on his master's degree in divinity. That's a miracle to me: that a man can go from extremely wicked to extremely righteous.

I could go on and on. I know how these guys were before. To see how they are now, that's the greatest miracle I could receive.

NEVER WAVER IN YOUR FAITH
IN THE FATHER

The LORD watches over the strangers;
He relieves the fatherless and widow;
But the way of the wicked He turns upside down.
Psalm 146:9 NKJV

My wife, Sara, and I met a Serbian named Vaso Bjegovich when I joined the Packers. Vaso owned a limo service, and we would ride in his limo when I did autograph sessions in Milwaukee. So we talked off and on, and we had the opportunity to lead him to the Lord two years ago.

Vaso took in a kid whom I had met a long time before at a group home in Pottstown, Pennsylvania. I hadn't seen the kid in years, but I believe the Lord sent him to us for help. He had spent years in and out of foster homes and prison before he had ridden from Pottstown to Milwaukee with a girl and gotten stranded there with no money. Vaso asked me to minister to them, and I did. Then Vaso asked me, "I want to open my heart to God, but what do I do?"

I said, "Vaso, continue doing what you're doing. By helping kids like this and giving them jobs, you're doing more ministering than most churches are."

He really committed himself to the Lord, and I baptized Vaso, the kid, and the girl on top of the roof of the Pfister Hotel.

About a month after we won the Super Bowl, Vaso brought a twenty-five year old to listen to me preach at Capital Christian Center in Milwaukee. A former gang member in Milwaukee, he told us about his being shot, which made him consider changing his life. He realized his old family life and gang life weren't worth it anymore.

I told Vaso, "Man, you've got to stay in touch with him. You've got to be his friend."

Well, Vaso stayed in touch. They became real good friends. Two or three months later, Vaso called and said the young man wanted to talk to me. The young man told me he had gotten saved in front of a lot of his former gang. He gave me the honor of marrying him and his girlfriend. This young man's life has changed dramatically. The former convict and former gang member have reformed their lives and become street ministers for the Lord.

Now other gang members are getting in touch with Vaso. Vaso is helping one kid who came from a very rough background. He had held up his fifth-grade class and been in a group home for a long time. But now he's eighteen and has a job, and he's doing well.

People of all different ethnic and financial backgrounds are coming to Vaso's house for Bible studies. Blacks, whites, Hispanics, poor people, middle-class people, ex-gang members are all selling out for Jesus.

It's exciting to see. You look at what Vaso is doing and realize, "Man, this is what it's all about." I read the Valentine's Day card one kid gave Vaso. He said he appreciated everything Vaso had done for him, that Vaso had become the dad he's never had. He wrote, "Thank you, Dad."

Vaso, Sara, and I visited Children's Hospital in Milwaukee, and just before we left, a mother came to us and begged us to pray for her seventeen-year-old daughter. When we went in her room, the girl grabbed Sara and I by the hands and said, "You've got to pray for me. I've seen the devil and he's going to kill me."

She was waiting for us because she'd been telling people that, but no one believed her. All of us—Sara, Vaso, and I—believe what she saw was real. We believe the devil was telling her he was going to kill her. Her mom and dad didn't believe her. No one else did. They thought she was hallucinating, going crazy.

We prayed with her and she said she was afraid to die. Some masked men had broken into her house, and one shot her with a double-barreled shotgun. She was really distraught about it. We told her, "God has allowed you to live. You're alive. Take solace in that."

Once again I told Vaso, "You've got to stay in touch with this girl and her family."

Vaso did exactly what I asked him to do. A week or two after the girl got out of the hospital, I was down in Milwaukee and Vaso took me to her house. She had only known Vaso for that short time, but she sat right between him and me and laid in Vaso's arms and said, "You're my daddy."

We're realizing that what kids want more than anything is a father. In the last words of the Old Testament, Malachi 4:6 says, "And he will turn / The hearts of the fathers to the children, / And the hearts of the children to their fathers, / Lest I come and strike the earth with a curse" (NKJV).

Mothers provide love, but our children's hearts today need to be turned back to their fathers. The kids who did the movie *Reggie's Prayer* with me said, "You're like a dad to us." Both girls and boys want fathers. God is moving us to give kids an opportunity to have a dad, even though that man may not be living with them, even though he may not be their birth father. God is moving us to show these hurting children who the real Father is. Because no matter how troubled they are, He can save them if they just put their faith in Him.

PART THREE

THE BOOK OF
KNOWLEDGE

MODEL YOURSELF
AFTER HEROES

Listen to counsel and receive instruction,
That you may be wise in your latter days.
Proverbs 19:20 NKJV

Every weekday my grandmother, Mildred Dodds, got on the bus and went to work. Every Sunday, no matter how tired she was, no matter the weather, she walked to and from church. Didn't matter if it rained or snowed. Didn't matter if she had to bundle up against the freezing cold or fan herself on a dripping-sweat muggy morning.

Maybe memory exaggerates, but if I'm not mistaken, her church was somewhere between three and five miles away.

That's a long walk for a grandmother. Hey, for anybody. Her example inspired me. The year I lived with her, the church bus came to take us kids to Sunday school, and she would walk to the church service a little later. Mildred Dodds was a clean-living lady. She talked about God, but she didn't force her faith on me, my brother, or my cousins. She didn't demand that we go to church, at least not in words. She demanded it with her actions.

Really, she taught me what commitment is all about. She had a deep spiritual commitment, and I wanted the same type of commitment—not just going to church but allowing God to deal with me in a powerful way. The year I lived with her, she made me more aware of what God wanted and who He was than maybe anybody.

My grandmother was my hero in the faith. My middle school coach was my first male hero. Leon Tyler was very stern and demanded more out of you than maybe you wanted to give. I used to think he was a mean man, but I realized as I got older that he was a caring man. But my number one male hero was my high school coach, Robert Pulliam. Coach Pulliam was single, and I could go to his house and we would just talk and talk. He pushed me harder than anyone ever had, but I knew it was because he cared. He played as important a part in my life as anybody.

I had more distant sports role models too. I wanted to tackle O.J. Simpson, shatter Hank Aaron's home run record, swoop through the air like Julius Erving, and share my Christian testimony like Bobby Jones.

O.J. was just a momentary fascination, a player to be admired, a player who inspired me to play football. I didn't know whether Hank Aaron was a Christian, either, but he was a hero as a player, and he became even more of a hero when I watched him push on despite all the death threats he endured just because he was about to break Babe Ruth's home run record. Because he kept going, he gave other black athletes a chance to achieve their goals.

Julius presented such class on and off the court that I wanted to be like him. When I found out the great Dr. J had made a profession of faith in Christ, that just made it even more gratifying for me. He was someone I wanted to pattern my life after.

Sara and I got a chance to get to know Dr. J and his wife, Turquoise, and Bobby Jones in Philadelphia when they were playing for the Sixers and I was playing for the Eagles, but I first met Bobby when I was a sophomore in high school and he spoke at a Fellowship of Christian Athletes camp in North Carolina. After seeing him share his testimony and his commitment, I gained a lot of respect for him, and he became a godly hero for me.

But I think my ultimate sports heroes were Jackie Robinson in baseball and Marion Motley in football. If they hadn't persevered over the racism they faced, black athletes probably would not have had the opportunities we do today. Whites called Jackie vicious names, spiked him, relegated him to second-class hotels and meals. Marion Motley was kicked by white players, verbally and physically abused, and the referees did nothing to stop it.

Some of these sports stars were not just role models, who could be positive or negative influences, but true heroes, who were only positive influences. True heroes always stand firm. They ooze class. They differentiate themselves from everybody else not just in sports but in godliness.

I wanted to be a hero, so I sought out heroes and studied them. I imitated them and drew inspiration from them. One thing I learned is this: Even though I wanted to have a personality like Dr. J, even though I wanted to live a fitter life like Bobby Jones, even though I wanted to be as committed to what was right as Hank Aaron and Jackie Robinson, even though I had coaches like Robert Pulliam who got personally involved in making me better, I also needed someone I could imitate spiritually.

I didn't have that until I was an adult and God brought Brett and Cynthia Fuller and Jerry Upton into my life. So, if someone asks me who my true heroes are, they're Brett and Cynthia Fuller and Jerry Upton, because they helped me to walk uprightly. If you don't recognize their names, that's understandable. They're not sports celebrities. They're more important. They're ministers. As Psalm 101:6 implies, I've made the godly of the land my heroes.

STUDY GREATNESS

He who walks with wise men will be wise,
But the companion of fools will be destroyed.

Proverbs 13:20 NKJV

Pepper Rodgers was my first pro coach. He did not fit your image of a coach at all, unless your image is that of Oscar Madison from *The Odd Couple.*

Pepper would come to practice in the morning with his hair uncombed, no socks, looking as if he'd thrown on whatever clothes he could grab, as if he'd slept in a garbage can.

Every day we laughed and joked about the way he looked.

Finally, one morning, he decided to fool us.

Here's what the head coach of the United States Football League's Memphis Showboats wore to practice:

White starched shirt.

Black tie.

Black tux.

Black cane.

Black top hat.

Black dress shoes.

And no socks.

Pepper always kept us loose. He was not a hands-on guy, but he was a real motivator. He kept us ready to play. If ever there was a coach I had fun playing with, it was Pepper Rodgers. He loved what he was doing. Good coaches realize there are times they need to keep the team loose and times they need to keep the team on pins and needles.

Good coaches come in all shapes and styles and demeanors. Pepper was a Southern wit. My next head coach, the man I credit for getting me into the NFL, Marion Campbell, was a Southern gentleman. He never said anything bad about anyone.

Buddy Ryan replaced Marion my second year with the Philadelphia Eagles, and I really blossomed under his attacking "46" defense. Buddy was a Southern wit, too, but no gentleman. I'll tell you a story about Buddy's cursing a little later. For now, let me just say that even calloused pro football players would drop their mouths wide open when they heard Buddy lambaste his own players. He humiliated some people, and we didn't understand it, but we knew there was a method to his madness. When he assembled his guys—guys who understood his system, who worked hard, and could play—Buddy was an extremely caring man. He was like a father to us and even our wives, and we did everything we could for him.

Then I came to Green Bay and found Mike Holmgren, a San Francisco native who drives a Harley and likes to tell jokes. Mike is not exactly one of those laid-back California surfer dudes, though. Like a lot of players and coaches who won championships with the 49ers, Mike has a fierce desire to win.

Before we played the 1996 NFC championship game, I went to Mike and said, "The guys think you're uptight."

"Who, me?"

"Yes, you."

"Not me. I'm never uptight."

I said, "Yes, you are, Mike."

But one thing I love about Mike is that he will listen to his players. I think all good coaches do; they not only offer knowledge, they seek it.

Mike came to the team and apologized. He said, "Some

guys have told me I've been uptight. Even though I don't think so, I'm gonna calm down a little bit."

And he did. He didn't do a lot of screaming and hollering, and it really helped us. If a head coach is uptight for a big game, there's a good possibility the players will get uptight. He loosened up, and we beat the Carolina Panthers for the NFC title and the New England Patriots for the Super Bowl title.

Then in 1997 we were struggling when we reached our bye week. Most coaches give you two or three days off, but if you're struggling, they might give you just a day or two, thinking they need to ride you even harder.

Here's where our Harley rider became the Easy Rider.

And here's another example of why he's such a good coach: Mike realized we were mentally and physically fatigued, and he gave us the whole week off. That's the first time an NFL coach has done that, and it was one of the most brilliant moves I've seen by a head coach.

We needed it more mentally than physically. Because we had reached the Super Bowl in 1996, we had played and practiced a full month longer than the teams who missed the playoffs, and we were left with just a two-month break to rest and heal before our first minicamp. Three weeks later, we'd had another minicamp; a month later, another; and then one month later, we had training camp, five preseason games, and then seven regular-season games. It was nothing but football for twelve months, and even if you love football, sometimes you get tired of it.

I think Mike realized, *Man, we've been struggling for seven games. We need a mental rest. We need to get away from football.*

So he gave us a full week off, told us we could get as far away from football as we wanted, and we did. When we came back, we felt fresh mentally.

And we played our best ball of the year and steamrolled into the Super Bowl.

But head coaches aren't the only ones I've learned from.

Position coaches and teammates have shared a lot of wisdom too. For instance, in Memphis, Chuck Dickerson was my position coach and John Banaszak was a sage veteran who had played for Pittsburgh's Steel Curtain Super Bowl champions. They taught me there was more to pro football than I ever imagined. They taught me about football fundamentals and how to achieve my goals. They taught me moves.

John Banaszak had a move similar to Howie Long's club move. He couldn't quite teach it to me, but when I saw Howie Long do it, I realized it was the move John Banaszak had perfected, and I worked on it until I perfected it too. Now it's one of my signature moves, and I'm not ashamed to say it's a move I stole. Howie was one of the best defensive lineman I had seen and I wanted to imitate him in the way I played. And that's great. You want to imitate what the greats use successfully.

Great players watch other great players and try to steal their moves all the time, just like great coaches quickly "borrow" plays or formations that work for their peers. People copied Buddy's "46" defense for years. Probably a third of the NFL has copied Bill Walsh's offense. Even today, they're running Bill's "West Coast" offense everywhere from San Francisco to Green Bay to Philadelphia, even though—and you can trust me here—I haven't seen too much of the Pacific Ocean in those two places.

Great coaches can help make you great. Study greatness. Surround yourself with great people, whether they are coaches or parents, preachers or teachers. Learn from their lessons. Do your homework, not just in sports or school but in life.

Wise people cull the best lessons from the best teachers. Fools forget the past and ignore the masters.

PART FOUR

THE BOOK OF FOCUS

FOCUS LIKE A LASER BEAM UPON YOUR GOALS

> And when Peter had come down out of the boat, he walked
> on the water to go to Jesus. But when he saw that the wind
> was boisterous, he was afraid; and beginning to sink he
> cried out, saying, "Lord, save me!" And immediately Jesus
> stretched out His hand and caught him, and said to him,
> "O you of little faith, why did you doubt?"
> *Matthew 14:29–31 NKJV*

It was March of 1998, and we were leading a group of Christians on a tour of Israel. We came to a place called Masada, an ancient Roman fortress on top of a mountain. A buddy who competes in Ironman triathlons wanted me to jog up the mountain with him.

"Dave," I told him, "I'm not jogging up there. I don't know if I'll even walk up there, because it takes forty minutes to an hour, and I've got a bad back."

But the real reason was, I'm afraid of heights.

So Dave jogged up the mountain without me. I started thinking it would probably be good for me to walk up the mountain—until I got there and saw how high it was. I decided to ride the cable car to the top. I was a little afraid even though my wife and kids were reassuring me. Later Sara told me that walking might have been more taxing on the body, but it was more reassuring to the senses because you knew you had terra firma underneath you. On the cable car you dangled and lurched far off the ground, only a few slim wires separating you from a fiery crash and certain death.

So the cable car took us almost to the mountaintop. My wife and kids were so excited, they ran the rest of the way and left me holding onto the railing. Slowly I started walking the rest of the way up a few flight of stairs. But instead of just looking up and focusing on the stairs, I looked down to see how high I was.

And I saw just how far I would fall if I slipped.

Then I started getting dizzy.

Dizzy enough I had to sit down.

Dizzy enough I had to take the cable car back to the bottom.

I was only a couple of flights away from the summit, a couple of minutes away from the rare site we had all come to see, and I couldn't make it.

Back down the cable car I rode, my guts doing cartwheels, my heart throbbing, my mind praying this would be over fast.

Two nights earlier I had preached a message on fear, and now here I was, backing down because of my own fear. I didn't tell anybody, but I almost cried because I felt I didn't overcome my fear. Three old ladies were there and I asked them if they had gone up—and I really would have cried if they had said yes.

Some people told me, "Well, the height is just an imbalance that you're not used to." But I still couldn't handle that as an excuse. I was disappointed with myself. Instead of looking straight ahead, I had looked down and lost my focus. And because I lost my focus, I had to come down off the mountain.

Peter walked on water until he took his eyes off whom he was supposed to be looking at—Jesus—and he nearly drowned. I slipped because I took my eyes off what I was supposed to be looking at—the pinnacle—and so I failed too. I was lucky. If I had been climbing a treacherous mountain with ropes and axes, a single momentary lapse of focus would have cost me my life. Instead, it only cost me a little dignity.

Expert mountaineers learn to discipline their minds and bodies because they realize distractions can be disastrous.

We need to focus just as intently upon what we do, because when we lose focus on the calling in our lives, then we detour from the path we're supposed to be walking.

Ever since I was a teenager, I have focused on becoming a great football player and using my stardom as a platform for the ministry. Because that was my focus, I worked hard on the field, in the weight room, and even in the locker room. One of my Packers teammates, LeRoy Butler, says I call more meetings than Congress. I call them to keep everyone focused on our goals.

We always talk about earning a Super Bowl ring. But pep talks can start to sound the same, and even flashing a ring can too. So the night before Super Bowl XXXI, Mike Holmgren gave us a real tangible sign of what winning would mean. He walked over to a table draped with a blanket, whisked it away—and revealed a huge mound of green. One hundred thousand dollars in cash.

"Gentlemen," Mike said, "I want you to remember that this is what we get if we win this game."

Now, most of us make a lot of money. But not many of us make a hundred thousand dollars a game, and even fewer of us have ever seen that much money in cash before. Our eyes got big, and we got fired up.

The next day, we did not focus on how deep the water was, how high the mountain was, or how good the Patriots were. We focused on what we had to do to earn that cash and that ring. I'm not saying that's why we beat the Patriots, but I know it didn't hurt. And I know that if you focus on your goals, you can accomplish most anything.

MAP OUT A GAME PLAN
TO REACH YOUR GOALS

A man's heart plans his way,
But the LORD directs his steps.
Proverbs 16:9 NKJV

Our offensive players tell me they must learn more than one hundred plays during training camp. Before each game Mike Holmgren and his offensive assistants will study the opponent, decide which plays work best, and map out a weekly game plan. The day before the game, Mike will go over the list with Brett Favre and script the first fifteen plays ahead of time.

In our defensive playbook, we probably have fifty to seventy different coverages and alignments, and in each game plan, we'll have more than thirty different defenses. We have to learn not only all those defenses, but all the formations and plays the offense can run against us each week. You've got to learn what they may run everywhere between the one-yard line at their end of the field to the one-yard line at our end of the field.

So that's why we watch so much film and practice—to study those formations and strategies, to learn why we're in certain defenses, to know all the ins and outs. Of course, we also have to work on our techniques and study the techniques of the guy we line up across from—the way he may block, the way he steps out, what moves we might be able to beat him with and which ones won't work.

People think we make all that money for playing three hours on sixteen Sundays during the fall. But we work out pretty much all year long, and during the season we work six days, and I go in on the seventh day because I feel I need to be an example and work hard.

Our work week begins Monday morning between nine and ten. Some guys come in early for Bible study. Some come in early so the trainers and doctors can work on their injuries. Then we work out—just a light session to get the blood flowing to all those sore muscles—and we watch film from noon to about three. A fairly short day, because our bodies are usually beaten up from slamming into three-hundred-pounders the day before.

Tuesday is the players' day off, but the coaches spend Monday afternoon and evening and all day Tuesday studying that week's opponent and devising the game plans. The coaches work incredible hours, usually from six in the morning until ten at night.

We return to work on Wednesday for our two hardest days. The defense meets first, from 7:45 to 8:15 A.M. Then everyone attends special teams from 8:20 to 9 A.M. Then until about 10:15 or 10:30, we go over the game plan and watch film of the opponent. Defensive players walk through our assignments on the field from 10:30 until 11, and then we have a team walk-through from 11:15 to 11:45. We eat, get dressed, and get taped from 11:45 until 1:30, and then we go back to the field and run through plays—often with full-contact hitting and scrimmaging—until 3 or 3:10 P.M.. Then we'll watch film until about 4:30 or 4:45.

We repeat that schedule on Thursday, but on Friday we don't have to come in until 9 A.M. Some guys work out in the weight room before that, though. We'll meet until about 10:30, have a walk-through until 11, get dressed, then practice from 11:45 until 1:10 or 1:15.

Saturdays are short days. We meet and have special teams and we can go home by 11 A.M. That's for home games. For road games, we spend Saturday traveling. And then, whether the game is home or away, we have to report to a hotel that night and meet again for an hour or so.

You have to work before you can play in the NFL. It's like anything in life: you have to practice before you can excel. The old cliché, "Practice makes perfect," isn't quite right. It should be, "Perfect practice makes perfect." You can't just glide through practice; you really have to put your mind and body into every hour, every day. You have to practice so much that it becomes a routine, so natural that when you have a split second to diagnose a play, you just react. Because if you're trying to chase down Barry Sanders or Steve Young, he who hesitates has lost.

The same prescription holds true in life. The Bible gives us a game plan, and that game plan tells us what can help us live and what can kill us. Some people think the Bible's rules and regulations are too strict, but actually, God is doing exactly what a father does for his son or daughter. He tells us what we should do, and if we obey, we can become like Him and help other people to become like Him.

So the game plan is how to live like Him, how to obey our Father and avoid mistakes. His team is not limited to eleven guys on the field at a time. His whole plan is to get as many people as possible on the team.

My wife sees another analogy between football and faith. "God talks about how we have to know our opponent. We have to read the field," Sara says. "Satan does that. Satan knows the Bible. He knows his competition. He understands our game plan better than we do. That's why he can trick so many of us. It's up to us to overcome him by learning the knowledge and wisdom of the Scriptures. Whoever knows the most wins. That's how you can gird yourself with protection."

We can also protect ourselves through strength in numbers. If I stand by myself and you run into me, even as big as I am, you could probably nudge me. But if I have other people standing behind me, holding onto me and giving me a foundation, then you won't be able to move me. So, because the devil knows our game plan better than we do, we have to band together as a team that has practiced God's game plan over and over again.

PART FIVE

THE BOOK
OF WORK

WORK WITH
ALL YOUR HEART

Whatever you do, do it heartily,
as to the Lord and not to men.
Colossians 3:23 NKJV

When I was just a high school sophomore, Robert Pulliam told me I could be not just a great high school or college football player, but a great pro—if I just learned what hard work and toughness were all about.

"He was a nice Sunday school boy who wouldn't harm a feather," Coach remembered years later. "We knew if we ever got him to be intense, he'd be a holy terror. He played pickup basketball with me and some older guys. They'd victimize him and he wouldn't fight back. I got annoyed. I challenged him. Every time he played a pickup game, I made sure I was on the opposite team. I'd use roughhouse tactics to get him upset and frustrated, get him to stand up and bang inside with me."

Coach Pulliam was six feet two inches and 250 pounds, a former football player at the University of Tennessee, as strong and tough as they come. When he elbowed and shoved, it hurt. I was already six-four and 225 pounds, but I didn't have the mettle to match the muscle. I ran inside the locker room and broke down crying.

"We took a water break," Coach recalled. "Reggie was the

last guy to the fountain. I called him over and he was still wiping tears away. I told him, 'I don't care about you crying. I want to see you *fight.* If you think I'm going to apologize, we might as well go back and I'll beat you again.' Two weeks later, in a student-faculty game, there was a crucial battle for a rebound. Next thing I knew, I was *sailing over his head.* By the end of the year, I had to back off. It got too rough. He had gotten the point."

Here's the point I had missed, which a lot of baby Christians and nonbelievers tend to miss: a Christian *can* be both faithful and ferocious. In fact, he's called upon to work harder than anyone else. If you study the Bible, you'll find many passages about the perils of laziness and the benefits of hard work. Even in sports.

As Paul wrote in 1 Corinthians:

> *Do you not know that in a race all the runners run, but only one gets the prize? Run in such a way as to get the prize. Everyone who competes in the games goes into strict training. They do it to get a crown that will not last; but we do it to get a crown that will last forever. Therefore I do not run like a man running aimlessly; I do not fight like a man beating the air. No, I beat my body and make it my slave so that after I have preached to others, I myself will not be disqualified for the prize. (9:24–27 NIV)*

Coach Pulliam helped instill that toughness in me the first time he made me cry and didn't apologize. Toughness is not the same as meanness. I'm talking about the ability to take punishment, to absorb the hits, to push on against pain and exhaustion, to stay focused even when you're tired or losing or frustrated. A tough player is not stopped by those obstacles; he uses them to fuel himself to even loftier achievements.

Coach Pulliam was just one person God put in my life to help get me where I am today. He was my friend. Even though he was stern and kicked my butt when he needed to, I always felt comfortable talking to him about my problems. Sometimes I thought he took things too far, and I'd be mad at him for a day, but I always knew he cared about me, and I respected him.

Colossians 3:23 has been the most motivational, inspirational passage in the Bible for me as an athlete, particularly early on in my career. To me, it's about both setting goals and working hard. A lot of times people do their jobs to please themselves or other people. But Paul said we should do it with all our might as to God. You'll push a lot harder if you do it unto the Lord. You'll give it everything you have!

DEVELOP PHYSICAL AND MENTAL TOUGHNESS

Blessed are the meek,
For they shall inherit the earth.
Matthew 5:5 NKJV

People misunderstand this Scripture. If you look in the original Greek language of the Bible, the word that's translated as *meekness* does not mean weakness; it means controlled aggression.

A Christian must be just as aggressive as Jesus was. He was so aggressive as a preacher that people tried to kill Him. He was so tough, He was nailed to a cross, resurrected, and changed human history. Jesus was meek but stern in everything He did. That's the attitude I've tried to emulate: stern meekness.

Time after time, I have realized that if I don't show my toughness by running and lifting weights until my body is exhausted, I won't build my body strong enough to withstand injuries. When I was a junior at Tennessee, I sprained both my ankles, chipped a bone in my elbow, and pinched a nerve in my neck. Before that, I thought I could get by on ability alone. Once I started getting injured, I realized it takes more than ability.

The media criticized me as a junior, saying I was soft because I was a Christian. It wasn't Christianity that made me soft; it was laziness. I just hadn't wanted to put the work in. I remember God telling me, "You weren't successful this past year because you decided to be a follower instead of a leader. If you want to be a superstar, if you want to elevate your game, you need to be a leader, and you need to work when nobody else wants to."

My senior year, I didn't wait on anybody else. I ran, I lifted, and I found out the more I lifted, the more the other guys would too. That year I was Southeastern Conference Player of the Year, one of only two or three defensive players ever to earn that honor. Then I went to the United States Football League and went back to my relaxed old ways and got injured both years. I didn't work hard when I first went to Philadelphia, either, and I broke a rib.

Finally, I made a commitment and a promise to myself that I would never go through an offseason without working my butt off and being prepared coming into the season. From that point on, my career elevated. I realized if I wanted to be a leader and a Christian, I had to work that much harder than the next guy, particularly the young guys. If I wanted them to be great and to step up and help me win a championship, I had to let them see that even though I'm older, I still work harder than they do. Not too many people question my toughness anymore. In fact, *Inside Sports* magazine put my picture on the cover headlined "The NFL's Ultimate Warriors" and named me the toughest guy in the NFL.

Some people don't understand. When I was a dominating senior at Tennessee, the same media who called me soft the year before turned around and said, "Wait a minute. Christians are not supposed to be this punishing." I thought it was funny. It was like they were going to criticize my faith no matter how I played.

I think it's funny, too, when people think Christians are not supposed to go all out and knock a guy's chinstrap loose. They pay me to make plays. I can't do that if I hold back and say, "I'm a good Christian, I won't hit him hard." I don't want to hurt anybody, but if I do, it's part of the game, and sometimes it does benefit my team. If I have a chance to hit an opponent, I'm going to hit him.

That's my job. That's my duty. I feel I've been called by God to spread His Word, and the more glory I earn on the football field, the more people will listen, and the more I can spread His message.

I've read that the Rams traded Sean Gilbert because he became a Christian and that supposedly made him soft. Hey, Sean Gilbert is a tough, Pro Bowl-caliber defensive lineman. Just because we're Christians doesn't make us soft.

Other people have said I play like a demon in disguise. I disagree. I think I play like the Holy Spirit lives within me. If I played like a chump, nobody would have anything to say or do with me. I may be a big guy, but I've got a God who can wipe out Reggie White at anytime. How can I be a sissy when I'm serving a God like that? It takes a *man* to walk for Jesus, because the man or woman who walks for Jesus is going to be ridiculed. I've been harassed, had *spitballs* thrown at me, been joked about, and been called Preacher Boy because I carried a Bible. But I stood fast in my beliefs.

Here's another misperception that bugs me. The Bible preaches about turning the other cheek and loving those who hate you. Football coaches preach about being tough and intimidating and violent. People think there's a big contradiction between those two. For years I've been asked how an ordained minister could play such a violent sport, and I get personally offended when our game is labeled as violent.

Football is not violent. When a kid puts a gun up to another guy's head and blows it off, that's violence. When racists burn down a black church, as they burned down ours in Knoxville, that's violence. Our game is aggressive, not violent. We don't go out to kill each other. We go out to win. But you've got to be tough to win in football—and in life. You've got to have controlled aggression.

LEAVE THE GAME
AT THE STADIUM

> In vain you rise early
> and stay up late,
> toiling for food to eat—
> for he grants sleep to those he loves.
> *Psalm 127:2 NIV*

Here's the greatest lesson I've learned as an athlete: don't celebrate your accomplishments until the day you retire. I've seen too many players try to live off one great game and suffer through ten bad games before they have another great game. I've seen too many enjoy one great season but no more because they relaxed.

When you get the ring and the money and the fame you have dreamed about all your life, it's easy to get complacent. It's like Eddie Arcaro, the great jockey, put it: "Once a guy starts wearing silk pajamas, it's hard to get up early." But you have to fight human nature, because living on your reputation won't keep you at the top for long.

Look at Michael Jordan. He has six NBA titles and more spectacular highlight-show moves than any player who ever lived. But he wasn't always "Air" Jordan, flying through the air with the greatest of ease. He couldn't even make his high school team as a sophomore. But every morning at 7:30, he met the coach and practiced his skills, and he quickly improved and wound up a star at the University of North Carolina. Did he get complacent? No.

He was drafted after somebody named Sam Bowie, and even when he was winning scoring titles, he wasn't winning championships. So he kept working until he learned how to win, and today he is known as the fiercest competitor, biggest winner, and probably the best player in NBA history.

Or look at the Packers. Even after we won the Super Bowl, many of us would show up on Tuesday, our only day off, to work out and get a jump-start on studying film. I'm not saying that trading away your free time and family time like that is right; I'm just saying that's the type of commitment that winners will give.

Where do you draw the line between working too hard and too little? Good question. It has taken me years to understand how to balance the conflict between career and family.

I used to bring the game home, particularly when we lost. I didn't really take it out on Sara and the kids, but I isolated myself from them, and they would go somewhere else just to let me get over the hurt and the pain.

I remember after one bad loss, Sara told me, "I understand what you're feeling."

"Sara," I said, "you're crazy! You don't understand what I'm feeling."

But after a while I began to realize that she does. Maybe not physically, but emotionally and spiritually, she's feeling all the hurt. One of my Eagles teammates, Greg Brown, saw how I would let the losses eat me up, and he gave me some good advice: "You've got to stop taking the game home."

I listened, and I tried to do that. But when Dallas beat us in the playoffs and I knew my Eagles career was over, I came home really upset. I went to the bedroom and just lay on the bed, angry and frustrated and despondent.

Sara and the kids knew to stay clear of me. But my daughter

came in and called my name. I turned around and asked, "What is it, Jecolia?"

"Dad," she said, "always remember this: I love you."

It took a four year old to remind me what was really important in life. Jecolia let me know that I should not take my job too seriously, because I still had somebody at home I could lean on. So now I do my best to stop bringing the game home.

That doesn't mean my job means anything less to me. When I'm working, I expend every ounce of energy I can, and the game means just as much to me as anything in life. But now when the game's over, it's got to stay at the stadium. Coach is always talking about leaving everything you've got on the field.

Leave the game at the stadium.

Leave your work at work.

Sure, losses still hurt. Sure, I still bring home film to study. Yes, coaches want you to work hard, to keep business on your mind. But I think they also understand there's a time when you have to relax from the game and be a father and a husband.

Don't get me wrong. I have let football rule my life at times, and at times I have taken my focus off my family and have neglected responsibilities. But I did my best not to neglect all of them. If I allowed people to let me limit myself only to football, I probably would be divorced by now. And losing my family would be far more painful than losing a football game.

PART SIX

THE BOOK OF TEAMWORK

BUILD BONDS
WITH OTHERS

Now the body is not made up of one part but of many . . .
The eye cannot say to the hand, "I don't need you!"
And the head cannot say to the feet, "I don't need you!"
On the contrary, those parts of the body that seem
to be weaker are indispensable . . . If one part suffers,
every part suffers with it; if one part is honored,
every part rejoices with it.

1 Corinthians 12:14, 21–22, 26 NIV

People look at our quarterback now and see a superstar, winner of an unprecedented three straight Most Valuable Player awards, football's best passer.

But when I came to Green Bay five years ago, a lot of people didn't know how to spell Brett Favre's name, let alone pronounce it. Brett had left Southern Mississippi just two years before, had left the Atlanta Falcons just a year before that, and had just thirteen starts in his pro career. Still, I thought he could be something special, because I remembered the game we played against him in November 1992. I remembered hitting Brett so hard, his shoulder separated. I told myself, "Okay, he's out." But he came back. And threw for 275 yards. And two touchdowns. With a separated shoulder. And he beat us.

Nobody was hailing him as the NFL's next great quarterback,

but there was a lot of hullabaloo about my joining the team. Some people were calling me the best defensive end in history and wondering why I would join such a nondescript bunch.

I could have come in and said, "Look, man, I'm the greatest of all time. I want all the publicity. I want to go to the Pro Bowl." But I realized I had never won a championship, and I wanted one bad enough that I didn't care who got the publicity.

Here's what I told my new teammates. "Everybody's talking about me being the savior. Yeah, Reggie White could potentially go to the Hall of Fame, but I'm only here to do one part. If we're going to win, Brett Favre needs to step up as a leader and as a quarterback. We've got to realize something: Brett Favre is the man. This guy can take us to a championship."

And you know what? He did.

Anybody could see his arm. Not everyone saw his attitude. Brett didn't have any ego. He didn't think he was better than anybody else. He worked hard. He didn't sit back and wait on anybody to give him anything. He went out and got it himself— and that filtered through the team. When you realize which players are going to carry you to the top, you almost become a supporting cast to them.

To build a championship team, you have to find players who are not jealous of the other guys, who don't have individual agendas. Their whole agenda is what needs to be done for the team. They're not concerned with who gets the credit because they know if the guy next to them has a great game, they're going to win. An individual player cannot be great sixteen straight games. But the year we won the Super Bowl, we told each other, "Look, all of us have to have at least six great games if we're going to win this whole thing," and that's all we concentrated on. When I didn't have a good day, LeRoy Butler and Eugene Robinson had great days; when LeRoy and Eugene didn't have good days, Sean Jones and I had great days.

The Lord can do great things through those who don't care who gets the credit. Like the tiny amount of glue that can hold two large objects together, so too can a few people bond and create great strength. Call it bonding power or creative cooperation, synergy or teamwork, there is strength in numbers.

Teamwork is one of the most important lessons that football has taught me, and it's a lesson that will help me when I finish playing ball.

Reggie White can't do it himself. Neither can Brett Favre. Neither can Mike Holmgren—that's why he delegates work among fifteen assistant coaches.

Even Moses needed help. In Exodus 18, his father-in-law told him, "The work is too heavy for you; you cannot handle it alone" (v. 18 NIV). Jethro instructed Moses to teach trustworthy men God's decrees and laws so they could serve as judges for their peoples, with only the most difficult cases brought before Moses.

Even Jesus needed teammates. He recruited twelve disciples. He realized He couldn't be everywhere, so He sent them out to spread God's Word. And He sent them out two by two because He knew they needed help to execute the mission.

Paul told the Corinthians that the church needs all of its members' varied talents, just as the body needs each of its parts to function properly.

But if there's an institution in the world that is not doing a good job when it comes to teamwork, it has to be the church. Sunday morning worship is the most segregated hour in America. The church has just as many problems when it comes to prejudice and racism as any other institution in the world. We don't want to admit it, because we think we're God's children and we're moving in His direction. What we don't realize is that God didn't call us for *us*, He called us for His people.

The body of Christ doesn't have teamwork. You've got Catholics, Baptists, pentecostals, Presbyterians, charismatics, Methodists, and on and on and on. All these denominations have put God in their own boxes and said, "This is the way God is supposed to be." Yet if they look at the Bible, they'll understand what God is all about and how we are to present Him. We're supposed to be serving one God.

I got my license as a Baptist minister, but these days I usually go to independent churches. I don't and won't label myself, because once we start segregating ourselves, we're missing the whole point. I got ordained in a nondenominational church because it is there that I really got taught and filled with the Spirit. I left a denomination more than nineteen years ago, and, now, I love just going by the Word.

CONSIDER NO TASK
TOO SMALL

Whoever desires to become great among you shall
be your servant. And whoever of you desires to be
first shall be slave of all. For even the Son of Man
did not come to be served, but to serve.

Mark 10:43–45 NKJV

Perhaps you have heard the story found in John 13. Jesus rose
from the meal, took off His outer clothing, poured water into a
basin, washed His disciples' feet, and dried them with a towel
wrapped around His waist.

But have you ever stopped to think about what that story
means? Consider the times. Two thousand years ago, the disciples weren't wearing Brooks Brothers or Nikes. They weren't
walking paved streets and sidewalks. They weren't bathing daily
under eight-speed showerheads or soaking in Jacuzzi tubs. No,
they were wearing sandals, traversing the desert for days on end
without washing. Their feet were grimy, filthy, smelly.

To wash someone's feet was no small act. It was a menial
task, fit only for slaves and servants. The disciples didn't even
wash their teacher's feet, let alone expect Him to do so for them.

So when Jesus got down on His knees and washed their
feet, it was an act of true humility, an example of the selfless service that culminated in Jesus' death on the cross. Jesus told His

disciples that if their Lord and Teacher could wash their feet, then they "ought to wash one another's feet. For I have given you an example, that you should do as I have done to you" (John 13:14–15 NKJV).

So if Jesus, the Son of God, the greatest man in history, could wash the feet of His disciples, how can we balk when we are asked to do the dirty work? No job is beneath us if it advances the cause.

Let me give you a football example. A defensive lineman is often defined by his sacks. The more he gets, the more money he earns, the more praise he earns, the more perks he earns.

Now, I've collected more sacks than anybody in NFL history, but I'll be the first to tell you that sacks can be misleading. A great defensive lineman plays the run just as well as the pass, and I pride myself on being a complete defensive lineman. If I selfishly ignored my run responsibilities and just chased the quarterback, I could have twice as many sacks as I do now— but we wouldn't have won as many games. And many times I have not gotten official credit for a sack, but my coaches and teammates know I caused it. Maybe I beat my man around the corner and the quarterback stepped forward into the pocket and right into the arms of our defensive tackle. Or maybe I was double- or triple-teamed, allowing a teammate to go straight to the quarterback without getting touched.

A lot of our sacks come on stunts and schemes and loops, and if the coach doesn't put us in the right position or a teammate doesn't do his part, we won't make the play. If I run a stunt and I draw more people to me, the other guy can get the sack. I had just as much to do with that sack as he did because I opened it up for him. He might get the stat, but I have to remember this: if he's successful, I'm successful. I don't want to sound like an egomaniac here; quite often I've "earned" a sack because a teammate did his job.

Or look at offensive linemen. The only recognition they get is when they hold somebody. They hardly ever get any credit, but they play just as important or more important a part of making great running backs and great quarterbacks.

I have no use for teammates who put personal goals ahead of team goals and won't do the dirty work it takes to win championships. They talk about teamwork, but they won't commit to do what's needed to win. An example is in the preparation, not on the field. A lot of young kids come in and say, "I want to go to the Pro Bowl." But what they fail to realize is that the Pro Bowl, an individual honor, is not the destination. The Super Bowl is.

Some kids come in and they're just glad to be a Green Bay Packer or a Dallas Cowboy, not realizing there's a purpose for them to be on the team: to help the team win a championship. Or you might have an older guy who's just hanging on, trying to attain his individual goals. If someone else on the team is playing better than he is, he may get extremely jealous or envious and won't even speak to the guy.

If you play within the scheme without worrying about individual attention, money, or statistics, if you concentrate on what you need to do to help the team win, you'll also achieve your individual goals eventually. I'm sure championship teams have some selfishness, some jealousies, but champions focus on team goals and not how much money or recognition somebody else receives.

Champions put in the extra work. They serve their teammates. They serve God. They do the dirty work. They wash feet.

PART SEVEN

THE BOOK OF
COMMUNICATION

ENCOURAGE OTHERS

Death and life are in the power of the tongue.
Proverbs 18:21 NKJV

My son, Jeremy, was playing outside with our dog one day when he started hollering and screaming. He was making so much of a racket, he was interrupting the work I was doing inside, and I shouted for him to quiet down.

Jeremy ran inside, sobbing loudly, and sprinted up to his room. I went upstairs ready to scold him—until I saw his shirt. Taz had been biting at him, ripping open probably a dozen holes in his shirt. But he never would have told me if I hadn't gone to see what happened.

Since then I've apologized four times. I want him to know I was wrong. If I had known Taz was attacking Jeremy, I would have gone out there immediately to help him. I feel so bad, because I wasn't sensitive enough to realize something was wrong.

Last night I apologized three times, and he told me, "Awww, that's all right, Dad."

I told him, "Jeremy, it's not all right. I should have found out what was happening. I'm sorry."

I apologized again this morning. I think kids appreciate it when parents admit they're wrong. That helps with their ego.

It's easy to correct your children or employees when they do something wrong, easy to forget to compliment them when they do something right. But it is absolutely vital to praise them to build their self-esteem, to make them believe they can accomplish anything. A therapist wrote that it takes fourteen positive comments to overcome one negative. Of course, I wasn't thinking of that then, but I did apologize to Jeremy four times. You've got to be man or woman enough to admit when you're wrong.

You've got to be man or woman enough to build up your kids. You've got to know how to mold them, how to scold them. Because, as Proverbs 18:21 says, the tongue is a powerful tool. It can encourage or discourage. It can lift up or put down.

A child's attitude is shaped by the way his parents, mentors, and coaches raise him. If they always berate him, he won't have a good attitude, because he'll think he's as low as they say he is. But if they lift him up, he starts to think he can do almost anything.

And you've got to have a positive, can-do attitude to succeed in life. I like how a mother praised a little boy who loved to play with paint. "My mother said to me, 'If you become a soldier, you'll be a general; if you become a monk, you'll end up as the pope.' Instead, I became a painter and wound up as Picasso," Pablo Picasso said.

I can tell how much my kids love being complimented, and my wife and I try to do so as much as possible. I realize that to get my children to think rightly about themselves, I have to communicate with them. We encourage them even in the midst of disciplining them, even when they are not perfect.

Jeremy was in a Scripture-quoting contest the other day, and I could tell he was nervous. He forgot a little of the Scripture he was quoting, described what it meant to him, sat down and looked over at Sara and me and asked, "How did I do?" We told him, "You did well. Look, Jeremy, this is not about winning and losing. You learned this verse, you got up and talked, and we hope you implemented the verse in your heart." The important thing was, he made the effort.

I want him to believe in himself and in God. Because, as Philippians 4:13 says, if Christ is in us, we can do any and everything. That Scripture goes hand in hand with Matthew 19:26, which says that "with God all things are possible" (NKJV). If we follow God's playbook, we will see those Scriptures fulfilled.

My best coaches and teachers have been positive and enthusiastic. It's like a man named Don Ward said: "Enthusiasm is contagious. Start an epidemic." Or, like George M. Adams said: "We should seize every opportunity to give encouragement. Encouragement is oxygen to the soul." Or, like Joseph Joubert said: "Children have more need of models than of critics."

Sara and I encourage our children and each other as much as possible. I tell Sara daily how beautiful she is and what a wonderful wife and mother she is. And I let my kids know they're the best kids in the world. I tell Sara, "I thank God He gave me you and nobody else." Sara does the same for me. She tells me how much she loves me and how handsome she thinks I am, how wonderful a husband and father I am. We don't do it just to say it, but because we mean it.

Of course, some of my teammates used to say, "Sara looks *good*, and you're so *ugly*."

And I'd say, "Look guys, everybody in the world can think I'm ugly, but as long as Sara thinks I look good, I'm fine."

LISTEN
BEFORE YOU ACT

The first one to plead his cause seems right,
Until his neighbor comes and examines him.
Proverbs 18:17 NKJV

This proverb was supposed to remind judges to listen to both sides of a case before drawing a conclusion. And it reminds me to listen before I act.

I forgot that when the dog was biting Jeremy. And I forgot it one day when my nephew was visiting and told me Jecolia had smacked him. We've raised our kids not to hit people and not to lie.

I asked her, "Did you smack Wesley?" and Jecolia said yes. I gave her a whupping, and when I say a whupping, I mean I spanked her with a belt. Afterward we sat down and talked about the episode.

"Where did you hit Wesley?" I asked.

She said, "I slapped him on the ankle."

I had assumed she had smacked him hard in the face. I checked a little more and found out it *was* just a light slap on the ankle.

I said, "Jecolia, you should have told me. I would never have whupped you if I'd known you just touched him on the ankle.

I tell you what. To prove I'm sorry, I'm going to get you something really, really special."

Well, months went by, and I flat-out forgot. So one day we were in the mall and Jecolia saw a cat and said she wanted it.

"We're not getting another cat," I said.

"Daddy," she said, "you remember when you promised you were going to get me something special? I want this cat."

When your little girl puts it like that, what's a dad to do?

"Okay, Jecolia," I said. "You got the cat."

We bought the cat and brought him home, and every day our keepsake cat walks around our house, pounces on visitors, jumps in our laps, and pesters us for food and play.

He is a living, breathing, daily reminder that if I do something wrong, I have to apologize and make it right. I can't be an arrogant father who thinks he's right all the time. Jeremy and Jecolia have to know their dad can say, "I'm sorry."

Jecolia calls the cat "Tiger."

I call him my "I'm Sorry" cat.

TELL THE TRUTH

> Then Jesus said to those Jews who believed Him, "If you abide in My word, you are My disciples indeed. And you shall know the truth, and the truth shall make you free."
>
> *John 8:31–32 NKJV*

When I was a kid, I used to lie.

I remember when I was nine, my friends and I would go to this store and steal Jell-O. We'd mix it with water and thought it tasted like Kool-Aid.

Well, the store told my aunt I'd been stealing. She confronted me, but I denied it. And the next thing I know, I see her walking over to my grandmother's place to tell her I'd been caught stealing. And who's walking right behind her but all my Jell-O stealing friends. The same ones who helped me steal it were the same ones coming to the house to see me get in trouble.

Lying and stealing backfired on me big time. I had to stay in bed the rest of the day without dinner. I was ticked too. I was already a big kid with a healthy appetite. I didn't want to miss dinner.

I'd like to say that was the last time I lied or stole anything, but that would be a lie, and I don't lie anymore. I stole comic books, and that backfired on me because my mom threw them away. I stopped stealing because I knew I'd get caught sooner or later.

I didn't stop lying until after I'd been married for two years. Sara would go to games and ask me why women in the crowds were looking at her. She asked if I knew them, and I said no, which was a lie. Finally, I told her I did know those girls and used to date some of them. It took two years before I realized that if I wanted to save my marriage, I had to stop lying to my wife, and stop lying in general, because lying does nobody any good. I think lying to your spouse is worse than cheating, because when you lie, it tears up a man or woman more than committing an act of adultery.

Read Jeremiah 9 and you'll see just how much God despises liars. The Lord laments over people who bend their tongues like bows, deceiving their neighbors and refusing to speak the truth. "Through deceit they refuse to know Me," He wails. "Shall I not punish them for these things? . . . Shall I not avenge Myself on such a nation as this?" (vv. 6, 9 NKJV).

Finally, I realized how much I had sinned, and I have not told a lie since 1988. You remember the scene from the movie *A Few Good Men* where Jack Nicholson is testifying at a military trial and Tom Cruise is badgering him? Nicholson tries to lie and cover up until he can't take it anymore and he finally bursts out, "You can't handle the truth!"

Well, now I will tell the truth, no matter what. Even if other people cannot stand the truth. Even if a little white lie would make them feel better. For instance, I'll have many people come up to me and say, "You remember me? You gave me your autograph two years ago when you were at so-and-so doing an autograph session." Well, they might have stood in front of me for ten seconds on a day when I signed a thousand autographs. I used to say I remembered them. But now I always tell the truth.

I think telling the truth is the most important part of being a coach or leader or father. What every player hates is a dishonest person. They despise coaches who lie all the time, who tell you what they'll do and then don't do it. When a coach is honest and does what he says he's gonna do, you'll give everything you have. It's the same with families. I can't tell my kids to be honest if I'm not.

Sara and I stress to our kids, "Don't ever lie to us." And our kids take it seriously. We've told them, "If you're honest, if you tell us you did something wrong before someone else tells on you, you'll get out of a lot of trouble." A few offenses demand punishment even if Jeremy or Jecolia tell the truth, but not many. I want to train them to be honest by any means necessary, and I started as soon as they were born.

When Jecolia was three, we were sitting at the table and she pinched her brother. Jeremy screamed, "Jecolia pinched me." I looked at Jecolia and she said she didn't. I told her, "If you lie to me, I'll whup you. I'll discipline you for lying." And as much as I didn't want to, I had to whup her for lying.

Jecolia has never lied since, and she's ten now. She's lied once or twice in her lifetime. I can honestly say that Jeremy has never lied once, and he's twelve. Funny though, some of his so-called friends know that he doesn't lie, and they try to trick him into lying. Sara tells him to just be who he is because they are upset at themselves for lying and they really do want Jeremy to be truthful.

For a while, my son took lying so seriously that he would tell on himself if he even had a guilty thought. During one training camp, he was calling me every day to tell me something like, "Dad, I was looking at a catalog and saw a woman in a swimsuit."

Every day! He kept doing this so much that one day I told myself, "I'm going to go home and tell him to stop this because he's wearing me out."

And the Lord spoke to me and said, "Why are you going to do that?"

I said, "Because he's telling me stuff he doesn't have to tell. This is just small stuff."

The Lord said, "If you do that, you'll be doing wrong."

"How?" I asked.

"You'll be teaching him to be dishonest. You tell him all the time that if he has a problem to talk to you about it. He's being honest with you."

Better to tell me everything than nothing. Better to tell the truth.

DO USE HUMOR

A merry heart does good, like medicine,
But a broken spirit dries the bones.
Proverbs 17:22 NKJV

Darkness was descending upon the Tennessee campus one night in the early 1980s. My coach, Johnny Majors, was talking to a reporter in the parking lot, one leg dangling outside his car door, when something clamped down hard on his leg.

The growl was so vicious, Johnny was convinced some deranged dog was about to tear off his leg.

Adrenaline pumping, he jerked his leg loose, rammed his leg inside the car, slammed the door, and, wide-eyed, stared out the window, searching for the menacing mutt.

It wasn't a German shepherd.

It was the Minister of Defense.

It was me.

Cut to 1985. Two reporters were chatting next to a table in the middle of the Eagles' locker room. On hands and knees again, I sneaked up behind Phil Anastasia of the *Camden Courier-Post*, put my mouth next to Anastasia's leg as if to bite it off, and growled.

The way he jumped up onto the table, you would have thought he was Michael Jordan.

Another unsuspecting victim fooled.

I began imitating dogs a long time ago. Started with Lassie. Eventually was able to growl like a little dog, a big dog, and an even bigger dog. I impersonated all sorts of celebrities too.

I discovered that once my football celebrity status lured listeners and my humor captured their attention and affection, then they would listen to my message. It's almost as if the laughter makes them trust you. I think we like comedians because they make us laugh and give us a sense of connection. Someone who's always serious, you're kind of skeptical about.

The Bible says a merry heart is like medicine, but a wounded spirit, who can bear it? If you can make the wounded laugh, then you can get into their lives and help mend their wounds.

Humor is extremely important. So I've learned that even while preaching, if I can get the crowd laughing, I get my message over a whole lot better than if I'm serious throughout the message.

When I used to address junior high and high school kids, I'd give more of a routine than a sermon. I'd tell how I used to hate to get up and go to school. Mom would come to wake me up and I'd stay in bed. Mom finally got tired of that, so she called in the U.S. Army. And I'd do sound effects, with the U.S. Army bringing in planes, bombs, the whole works. Kind of like Police Academy, only not as good. It went over big with kids.

But my routine has gone to the dogs. About three years ago, I realized most kids didn't know those people anymore. I'd be imitating Elvis Presley and Muhammad Ali and Clint Eastwood and pro wrestlers. Some recognized Ali or the wrestlers, but they didn't laugh. They have to know the whole cast of characters, because each builds on the other, or the routine doesn't work.

So I don't use impersonations much anymore except maybe for television. Now, I just preach and try to depend on the Spirit of God to give me something to say that will make the people laugh—and make them think about God.

But every once in a while, I still surprise 'em.

When we visited Israel in March, we were in the cave where they believe David passed up the opportunity to kill Saul. I saw a dog running through a stream in the cave, and I said, "Watch this," and I barked.

That dog looked right up, and we started laughing.

I barked again and he stopped and looked again.

I don't know if I mended or stopped that dog's heart, but I got a lot of people laughing. And you know what they say: Laughter is the best medicine.

DO NOT CURSE

Out of the same mouth come praise and cursing.
My brothers, this should not be.
James 3:10 NIV

Hollering is almost universal among football coaches, and quite a few sprinkle profanity amid the screams. Most players are accustomed to it, and I can handle the screaming and hollering, but not the cursing. It actually motivates some guys, but to me, some words are just foul and humiliating, and they just rob me of the effort I want to give. If a coach curses, that shuts me down immediately, and I'm not shy about telling him.

When I went to Tennessee, Johnny Majors was my coach and Larry Marmie was my defensive coordinator. I went to Coach Majors and said, "If you want to holler at me and make me run all day, I'll do it. The only thing I ask is that you don't curse." Coach Marmie heard about it and made a promise to the whole defense: "I will scream at you, but I will never curse or humiliate you."

Our attitude was, "Yeah, right. Let's see."

But he kept his promise. He screamed but he never cursed, and we went from number ninety-nine in total defense to number nine.

Then one day in Philadelphia, my defensive line coach

cursed. Even though Dale Haupt didn't curse at me, he did it in front of all the players, so I wanted to retaliate in front of everybody. I said something back, and we started yelling at each other.

I didn't curse, but I was wrong. You don't do that to your boss, especially when you're a Christian. I went to him the next day and apologized for confronting him in front of everyone, and I told him I didn't mind when he was mad and hollered and screamed, but cursing really offended my faith. He apologized to me, and I apologized to him, and it was over.

Well, almost over. Dale quit cursing, but nothing could stop Buddy Ryan from cursing. He just cursed in general, not at me. Buddy loved me, but asking Buddy to stop cursing was like asking him to stop breathing, so I just gave up trying, and I didn't even think about it anymore.

Until one night at training camp. Now, you have to understand, camp was forty-five minutes away from our homes, and we spent six weeks every summer sweating all day long, then cooped up in little cinder-block dorm rooms all night long. We didn't get many hours off, let alone days, and after being sequestered for a few weeks, it could drive a man crazy. So one night Sara was coming to visit, and I left my dorm room and went upstairs to ask Buddy if I could spend the night at a hotel with my wife.

I walked into an office where some of the assistant coaches were meeting and asked if Buddy was around, and they yelled down the hall, "Buddy, Reggie White wants you."

So here Buddy comes out of his room, clear at the other end of the hall, and he starts walking and talking.

"Reggie White," he hollers in that Oklahoma drawl of his, "I am not gonna stop cursing. I have been cursing my whole career. I can't stop now. You can't ask me to stop cursing. This is the way I talk."

He went on and on until he got right up to me.

And I said, "Buddy, I didn't come to ask you to stop. I came to see if I could spend a night with my wife."

Buddy was so relieved, he started laughing.

"Oh sure," he said. "You can spend the night with her."

Buddy never did stop cursing. But he knew how it bothered me. One time we played Indianapolis in a preseason game, and I didn't have to play the second half except for the field goal unit. I went in, and one of the Colts linemen cursed at me, so I went back to the sideline and told Buddy I wanted to play the second half after all because the guy cursed me.

He said, "Go in for one play."

So I went in, but we were using a defense where I lined up on the tight end instead of the tackle who had cursed me. Buddy told me I only had one play and since I couldn't get him, I ran up to him and told him, "Don't you *ever* in your life use profanity on a man of God again."

And he told me, "Reggie, I apologize. The guys on the sideline told me that you are a minister, and I'm sorry."

I was shocked that not only did he apologize but that his own teammates had chastised him and told him he was wrong.

Another time, a Detroit rookie used foul language that I would not let my dogs hear, and I looked him right in the eye and announced, "Jesus is coming back soon, and I hope you're ready." He just cursed me some more and returned to his huddle, and I was mad. I shouted across the field, "Jesus is coming back soon, and I hope you're ready." We broke our huddles, lined up a few inches from one another, and I said, "Jesus is coming back soon, and I don't think you're ready."

When the ball was snapped, I said, "Here comes Jesus!" and with every ounce of fury I had, I plowed into his chest and drove him back about five yards. He plopped to the turf just in time to see me sack his quarterback.

After that, whenever we needed a big play, Buddy would ask me if Jesus was coming back soon.

DO NOT BOAST

The tongue is a small part of the body, but it makes great
boasts. Consider what a great forest is set on fire by a small
spark. The tongue also is a fire, a world of evil among
the parts of the body. It corrupts the whole person,
sets the whole course of his life on fire,
and is itself set on fire by hell.

James 3:5–6 NIV

It was November 18, 1996, and we were playing the Dallas
Cowboys. They had eliminated us in the playoffs three straight
years, had beaten us six straight times. We knew if we were to be
the best, we had to beat the best, and we were frustrated we
couldn't beat the Cowboys, frustrated that each of those games
was played at Texas Stadium.

So we went to Irving, Texas, and this time we were going to
show the Cowboys, show our NFL brethren, and show fans
throughout the country that the Packers were for real. The
game was on ABC's Monday Night Football. Prime time. Big
time.

We did not allow a single touchdown. But Dallas kicked six
field goals and led, 18–6. The Cowboys were close enough to
kick another field goal, but only a few seconds remained, and
we were beat. Troy Aikman took a knee once to run time off the

clock. And he was about to do it for one final play when Barry Switzer sent Chris Boniol out to try for a record seventh field goal.

Troy waved him off and yelled, "Get outta here! We're running out the clock!"

The kicker shouted, "We're calling a timeout and kicking a field goal! That's what Barry wants."

Troy still wouldn't leave the field. "Get outta here! We're not kicking a field goal!" he shouted. But Barry started yelling at Troy from the sidelines, so Troy left the field, boiling mad, and Boniol kicked the field goal.

Then the cameras showed me jawing with Michael Irvin, and the announcers suggested we might fight. We weren't. Michael was just trying to calm me down and explain they were going for a record.

"Mike," I replied, "I understand what's happening, but it doesn't have to be done! You don't do that, even for a record. You already won the game, Troy was running the clock down, but Barry wants to rub our noses in it by kicking that field goal!"

Barry had dissed us before. He had gone on TV and gloated and said, "We kicked their —."

Good sportsmen don't do that. Good Christians don't do that. They show a little class. A little respect. They don't brag and gloat and rub it in.

It grieves me to see coaches and athletes boast about their victories, their accomplishments, and how great they are. They become self-centered and make themselves their own gods. You look at them and think, "This joker just doesn't get it. God created this opportunity for him, even though he's wicked." I've seen a lot of guys in my profession who just don't want to acknowledge that God gave them this ability. They think they created everything around them.

When you boast, you become arrogant and prideful. The Bible says pride goes before a fall. Once you get prideful, you will fall sooner or later. And fall hard. That's why we have to stay humble.

I take the advice of the apostle Paul. I don't boast in my abilities. I boast only in God's abilities. In many respects, I've accomplished more than other athletes have, but I understand my abilities have come from God Himself. That's what I boast about. Not my accomplishments. Not my talents. I boast about what God has given me and what He's done in me because I know everything I have came from Him. And I have to be able to use His gifts to give back to others, so their talents and their abilities will come out as God wants them to come out.

Joe Gibbs understands this. Joe coached the Washington Redskins to four Super Bowls, winning three, in just a dozen years. But at Joe's induction speech at the Hall of Fame, he credited God again and again.

And when he talked on NBC about the Cowboys rubbing it in, he remembered one time his Redskins got me mad. "We're playing Reggie in Philadelphia and he knocks our quarterback all the way past us, underneath the Gatorade bench on our sideline," Joe told NBC viewers. "He's right there and we're calling him all these names and then we go to Hawaii to coach the Pro Bowl. Reggie gets on the bus a little late, walks halfway down the aisle until he reaches our coaching staff, and says, 'I remember what you guys called me on the sideline.'"

And Joe turned to the camera and concluded, "I've got a feeling the Cowboys are going to be sorry they kicked that field goal."

We didn't play the Cowboys again that year. The Carolina Panthers beat them in the playoffs before we got the chance. But we beat the Panthers to win the NFC title and beat the Patriots to dethrone the Cowboys as Super Bowl champions.

Our next game against the Cowboys was almost exactly a year later. It was November 23, 1997, and this time, we finally got them at Lambeau Field. And we crushed them, 45–17. We held the Dallas offense to just one touchdown, and Dorsey Levens had nearly as many yards as all the Cowboys combined.

We went back to the Super Bowl, and Barry Switzer went home to Oklahoma. The Cowboys collapsed to 6–10, and we went 13–3 again. Barry got fired, and we got another NFC championship.

PART EIGHT

THE BOOK OF CHARACTER

DO NOT TAKE REVENGE

Repay no one evil for evil. Have regard for good things in
the sight of all men. If it is possible, as much as depends on
you, live peaceably with all men. Beloved, do not avenge
yourselves, but rather give place to wrath; for it is written,
"Vengeance is Mine, I will repay," says the Lord.
Romans 12:17–19 NKJV

I know I was supposed to leave vengeance to the Lord when we
played the Cowboys in 1997, and I know I was not supposed to
seek revenge when I played my first game against the Eagles in
1993.

But it is human nature, and I am human. I was mad at the
owner, Norman Braman. I was mad at the coach, Rich Kotite. I
was mad at management. I know how hard I worked for that
team, how much effort I put in. I know I deserved the money I
was paid. And when I left Philadelphia for Green Bay, not only
was Norman telling me I didn't deserve the money, he even
convinced some of the public that I didn't deserve it. After realizing what Norman believed in and how he is, I had to forgive
him because he didn't know any better.

Buddy Ryan put together a team with talent, and he put us
through some incredibly hard training camps. But Norman
wouldn't pay the players to keep us together. He was making

about ten million dollars every year off the Eagles—various studies showed he was earning as much as any owner, and that doesn't even include the way the team's value appreciated—and yet he was always trying to nickel-and-dime players, and guys would be forced to miss weeks of football.

Norman was more interested in making money than winning games. We worked hard, and we wanted to win bad, but we saw ownership wasn't giving the effort to try to help us win it all, and frankly, it ticked off a bunch of us. It made me mad. It made me bitter.

Norman just refused to treat people right. Even his stars. I'll give you an example. Mike Quick was one of the greatest receivers in Philadelphia history. When Mike retired, the organization gave him a golf bag and golf clubs worth a thousand dollars, and half-dressed cheerleaders came out and thanked him for everything he had given to the Philadelphia Eagles. Mike Quick had the sorriest retirement send-off I've ever seen. He deserved much more than that.

I don't think ownership was focused on the same goals as the players, and when you have lack of focus from the top, it filters through the team. We never gained focus because some players had problems with other players and their lack of focus. We knew Norman was going to get rid of Buddy, but when Buddy benched Randall Cunningham for a series in the playoffs, Randall sold out Buddy by refusing to support him publicly, and that made most of the players mad.

I loved Philadelphia, and it grieved me to leave. But Norman didn't make much of an effort to keep me, and when I signed with Green Bay, he mocked me. He said I didn't follow God, I didn't go for the inner city, I went for the most money. Norman didn't know what was in my heart. He didn't know what was in God's heart. But God knows *his* heart.

So when we played the Eagles in September 1993, just a few months after all this happened, I wanted to beat them really bad. I wanted to get back at Norman; I know Norman wanted to get back at me. I know Rich Kotite wanted to get back at me, and I was a little upset with Rich because he hadn't stood up for me or the other guys.

I had eight tackles, forced two fumbles, and collected a sack. But we lost by three points, and it really devastated me. I thought we had a good enough team to beat them, but we didn't.

If we had won, I would have gloated in vengeance, just as Norman gloated when they won. I think God wanted us to lose so I wouldn't gloat and so I wouldn't take all the glory for myself and take pride in beating Norman Braman and not the Philadelphia Eagles.

So, as natural as revenge is, I had to repent from that attitude. We shouldn't take revenge on anybody. We shouldn't repay evil for evil. In 1 Corinthians 13, it talks about that: don't rejoice in evil but in the truth (v. 6).

A lot of times we will rejoice when something bad happens to someone who has done us wrong. So I know I'm not supposed to rejoice, but I do ask God to judge people, as well as myself, because judgment brings about righteousness, and our purpose is to see people saved and to see them grow.

I've had some good games yet just one victory in four tries against the Eagles. But the losses no longer devastate me. I think God has shown judgment on that team because of the way Norman treated us.

When Norman started messing with us, he brought judgment against that team. I didn't repay evil for evil. The Lord did.

PRACTICE FORGIVENESS INSTEAD OF REVENGE

> For if you forgive men their trespasses,
> your heavenly Father will also forgive you.
> But if you do not forgive men their trespasses,
> neither will your Father forgive your trespasses.
> *Matthew 6:14–15 NKJV*

My mother, Thelma, was fifteen when she bore my brother, Julius, and nineteen when she gave birth to me. My dad, Charles White, never married her, never lived with us. Thelma was a single parent until she married my stepdad, Leonard Collier, when I was seven.

I saw my dad maybe once or twice a year, when his professional softball team came to town and I would go to his games. That was a highlight for me because I enjoyed watching him play and spending time with him. Deep down inside, I wanted to love him.

And yet I also wanted to hate him because he wasn't around. I wanted to be bitter, but the times I did see him, he didn't do anything to make me resentful. If he had been rude and arrogant and disrespectful, maybe I would have been bitter, but he wasn't any of that.

Did my father neglect me? There's neglect whenever people have kids out of wedlock; there has to be responsibility when it comes to having sex. The neglect continues when they don't get married and don't stay together.

But that doesn't mean my parents didn't love me. They were caring people. My mother did the best she could to raise me. And my dad was good to me when he was around. I believe he loved me, and I loved him. I loved telling people he was my dad, because he built a good reputation. He was a great baseball and softball player, an excellent athlete, a good man. I tell my dad often nowadays, "Man, everywhere we go, more people know you than me."

It would have been nice to have a man, a father, around to help me. I probably wouldn't have done some of the things I did. I would also be better off domestically! Charles is one of the cleanest, neatest men I know. But I didn't have a man I could really talk with until I met Coach Robert Pulliam in high school.

I used to be bitter and mad, but when I got older, I evaluated my own life and realized I had had premarital sex, too—he had children as a result, and I didn't—so how could I condemn my father? I had to forgive him.

The greatest power we possess is forgiveness. If we are able to forgive those who have hurt us, it advances our spiritual growth more than anything else can. Revenge is natural. Forgiveness is spiritual. People say revenge is sweet. The Lord says, "Vengeance is Mine." When you forgive and trust God to repay evil, you display reverence. It doesn't mean you think the sinner was right; it means you trust God to do what is right.

You might think, "Oh, God is busy with other things. Let me get even with this guy myself. What good will it do me to forgive and let him get away with hurting me?"

Here's what good it will do. If you forgive, forget, and focus on the positive, your mind, heart, and soul will feel much better than if you carry around all that anger and pain and vengeance. They are cancers, gobbling up your spirit like Pac Man. Maybe you can't change the sin, but you can change your emotional response to it.

When you forgive the people who have hurt you, who have abandoned you, who have forgotten you, you eliminate grief and gain contentment. Forgiveness moves us into a love relationship even with those we have hated.

Look at the Bible. A number of great men sinned. Paul killed Christians for a living. David was the king of Israel and a man after God's own heart, but he killed a man and committed adultery. Moses killed a man. Gideon was a poor man, but God used him to lead Israel against the Midianites. You look all through the Scriptures, and you see hard-core, wicked folks. But God forgave them, changed them, and made them right.

In Jesus' Sermon on the Mount, He asked, "Why do you look at the speck in your brother's eye, but do not perceive the plank in your own eye? How can you say to your brother, 'Brother, let me remove the speck in your eye,' when you yourself do not see the plank that is in your own eye? Hypocrite! First remove the plank from your own eye" (Matt. 7:35, paraphrased).

I dial up my dad even today, and we talk. I forgive his mistakes, just as my Father forgives mine.

DO NOT JUDGE
NON-CHRISTIANS

Judge not, and you shall not be judged.
Condemn not, and you shall not be condemned.
Forgive, and you will be forgiven.
Luke 6:37 NKJV

My stepdad and I did not get off on the right foot when my mother married him. The first year they stayed in Kansas while Leonard finished his army hitch, and my brother and I stayed in Chattanooga with my grandmother.

When they got back, the first time my grandmother called my mother and told her I was disobeying her, my stepdad came over and whupped me. I probably deserved the whupping, but I didn't appreciate it. Not by this intruder in our lives. Not when he didn't even sit down and talk to me about it. He came in with the attitude that it was his way or no way, which it should have been, but I couldn't accept it back then.

My stepfather started drinking and over a period of time became a heavy drinker. He drank constantly—close to every day—and he stayed intoxicated a lot. I was trying to be a good Christian, and I didn't think drinking was right. I didn't like him and I didn't like his stepping in the way he did. I was bigger than he was, so I won some of our scuffles.

I realize now I was taking away his authority as a man and

father. The more he drank, the more and more judgmental I became. I thought the church was teaching me to judge him, because he wasn't doing what God wanted him to do.

The thing I wish I'd realized then is that the Bible tells us to righteously judge those who are in the body of Christ and have sinned. We should not judge the ones who are outside the church; God will take care of them. So if I'm telling a non-Christian he's wicked and no good, I'm judging him. Maybe he is no good, but I must realize that only God can handle him. I can tell him until I'm blue in the face that he needs to change his life, but the Bible says a wicked man does not perceive spiritual things. I cannot righteously judge a man who doesn't know God, because only God can change him.

If I could go back and do it right this time, I would have just said, "Lord, I'll let you take care of this. This is my stepfather and I'm going to love him no matter what. I'm going to trust You to change him. I'm not going to put any pressure on him."

Back then, I was bitter. Today I'm not. He drank too much, but Leonard was a good man. He was a provider. He loved my mother. He loved my sister as his daughter. And I think as I got older he loved me just as much. When I got into twelfth grade, we became a lot tighter; I understood him, and he understood me. I probably got most of my humor from my stepdad; he was a funny man. He was fun to talk with, fun to wrestle with.

Sometime after Thanksgiving in 1992, I told my wife, "Sara, I need to call Leonard. I'm gonna tell him how much I love him and care about him. This year I'm going to start spending some time with Leonard."

I said maybe we should go fishing after the season, and she pointed out I never fish. I knew that, but Leonard liked to fish, and I wanted to do something he liked and tell him I was sorry for how I had treated him.

Not long afterward, police found Leonard Collier dead in his car, killed by a hammer to the head. I'll never forget the date. It was December 19, 1992, my thirty-first birthday.

When Sara told me he was dead, it really broke my heart because I hadn't had a chance to sit down and be nonjudgmental and become a friend. Not only his friend, but his son. If I regret anything in my life, I regret that I spent more time judging him than loving him.

His death was hard for me to take, and it still is, because I often dream about him and some of the times we had. I dream we have that time to talk now.

But we cannot, and we never will.

I beg of you now: Please, please don't make the same mistake I did. Stop judging the people in your lives. Reconcile with them. Show them you love them.

Now.

Before it's too late.

Before you're sorry.

STOMP OUT RACISM

The Jews answered and said to Him, "Do we not say
rightly that You are a Samaritan and have a demon?"
Jesus answered, "I do not have a demon; but I
honor My Father, and you dishonor Me."
John 8:48–49 NKJV

I own a forty-five-foot bus—so big it looks like a tour bus—
and Sara and the kids and I drove it down to Disney World. On
the way home we were going to stop at the home for young boys
run by Mel Blount, a Hall of Fame cornerback for the great
Pittsburgh Steelers teams of the seventies. We were on a route
from Jacksonville, Florida, to Mel's place in Vidalia, Georgia,
when a state trooper drove up beside me, looked in the bus, and
fell back and started following me.

I told Sara, "I'm going to get pulled over."

She said, "For what?"

I said, "This cop just looked in. He wants to know who's in
this bus. I know he does because he sees a big black dude driving this big luxury bus."

After about thirty minutes, the cop put his lights on and
pulled me over.

So I got out and said, "Officer, what did I do?"

I wasn't speeding because I knew he was behind me.

He said, "Well, your speed was going up and down."

"It was going up and down," I said, "because every time I went into a small city, the speed limit was lower, and when I went outside the small city, the speed limit went up."

"I need to see your license and registration," he said.

I went to the bus and told Sara, "He said he stopped us because our speed varied, but I think what he really wants is to know who's in this bus."

So I gave him my license and registration, and Sara came out and got a little hot. She told the cop, "Can we see the radar to see how fast we were going? I think you really stopped us because we're black."

He said no.

She said, "By law, you have to let us see it." If they're going to charge you with speeding, they do have to let you see the radar. But the cop still refused.

"Sara, get on the bus," I said. I knew this cop could do anything he wanted, then claim we provoked him; it was a black man's word against a Southern cop's. So Sara got back on the bus and got out our camcorder, filming everything just in case.

He looked at my license and registration, and I think he recognized my name but tried to act like he didn't. "Well," he said, "you can go now. Just slow down."

"I wasn't speeding anyway," I said, and I got on the bus really ticked off.

Maybe whites think blacks are paranoid, but if whites were presumed guilty until proven innocent, if they got pulled over, delayed, hassled, and abused as often as we do for DWB—driving while black—then they would be infuriated too.

Mine is no isolated example. Poll some successful black men and you'll see. If they drive nice cars, chances are they've been pulled over by cops when they did nothing wrong. And more than once. White cops have told me, "Yes, Reggie, we do profile. We're trained that if we see a black man in a nice-looking car, we're supposed to pull him over."

When I was in Philly I got pulled over once because I was in a Mercedes. Actually, I didn't see a sign that said you couldn't turn right on red, and a cop pulled me over. But he didn't say anything about my turning right on red. What he said was, "Why are you driving a car like this?" He figured a young black guy driving a Mercedes must be dealing drugs.

When I said, "I'm Reggie White," he apologized to me. But if I had not been a celebrity, he would not have apologized, and he would have continued to interrogate me. I know if I were just a normal black guy, I would have gotten a ticket and may be beaten up. White people sometimes tell me, "Reggie, you shouldn't get mad over the Rodney King verdict. You're a Christian." I'm still black, though. Or they say, "You shouldn't be mad about the things that have happened to your people in the past."

You can't tell me not to get mad at injustice because I'm a Christian. I get mad *because* I am a Christian. Jesus got mad at injustice—not just for His people, but for the Gentiles and Samaritans too.

Back then, Jews hated Samaritans. The people of Samaria were of mixed blood, a race resulting from marriages between Israelites left behind in the exile and Gentiles brought into the land by the Assyrians. But even when the Samaritans began to follow the teachings of Moses, the Jews looked down on them and didn't associate with them. To single one out as "a good Samaritan" was a rarity, just like a racist redneck being surprised to discover "a good nigger."

But who was the first person Jesus told that He was the Messiah? A Samaritan woman. If you read John 4, you'll see her testimony led many Samaritans to befriend Jesus and become believers even while many Jews persecuted Him.

If Jesus didn't judge people based on their heritage, why should we? Don't dishonor Him, and don't dishonor others with prejudice.

BE RESPONSIBLE AND ACCOUNTABLE FOR YOUR ACTIONS

A bishop then must be blameless, the husband of one wife,
temperate, sober-minded, of good behavior, hospitable,
able to teach; not given to wine, not violent,
not greedy for money, but gentle, not quarrelsome,
not covetous; . . . not a novice, lest being puffed up with
pride he fall into the same condemnation as the devil.

1 Timothy 3:2–3, 6 NKJV

When I was a high school senior, a young pastor at St. John's Baptist Church told the congregation that God had called him to preach. I started wondering if God was calling me to preach. One day I decided that He had, and I became a licensed minister in July 1979.

I don't know how they did it in white Baptist churches, but in black Baptist churches, ministers from other churches came and listened to you give a trial sermon, and if they approved, they signed your license. That's how it started for me. I preached before the ministers, the whole congregation, and all my friends and family. I was extremely nervous. I'd never spoken before people in my life. But I felt God's call on my life and I *had* to do it.

So I became a minister at seventeen, but 1 Timothy 3 gives the qualifications of a bishop or minister, and it also says he must not be a novice or a new convert. Which I was. I'd only been saved for four years. Scripture says a new convert who preaches may be convicted for his pride and fall into the condemnation of the devil.

That's what happened to me. I allowed the devil to deceive me because I was unlearned, I didn't get any discipleship, and I didn't have any accountability. The devil did exactly what he wanted to do with me. I became spiritually proud. If Billy Graham and I were sitting in the same room witnessing to people, I figured Billy needed to shut up and let Reggie talk. That's how prideful I was.

None of us is perfect, but while I was in college, I was a minister sleeping around. I'd have sex with a girl one night and the next morning I'd preach. Of course, I'd feel bad about it, but I finally realized I needed some discipleship, some accountability, somebody to tell me when I was wrong. Somebody to tell me, "Hey, man, you need to stop." I didn't need the people who said, "That's all right, everybody does it."

Praise be to God that He gave me some accountability when I was twenty-six. That's when I allowed people to come into my life who would watch over my ministry and work with me. That's when my life really began to change.

I started to change in college under the discipleship of my pastor and best friend, Jerry Upton. But when I was twenty-six, Brett and Cynthia Fuller, who are pastors in Washington D.C., helped me to understand that I needed to get discipled, I needed to get into the Word, I needed to understand what ministry was all about.

So I stopped preaching for a year and studied the Bible and got the discipleship I needed. During that year the Lord began to show me I needed to take the gospel into neighborhoods where people were oppressed and hurting. I began to realize what ministry truly was: helping those who needed help the most.

Gradually I began to realize I had to be responsible for my

own actions. I couldn't change my past, but I could rise above it. I couldn't blame an absent father, an alcoholic stepfather, or wicked women, but I could silence my voice long enough to listen to God's voice. I couldn't choose my parents, but I could choose my mentors. I chose God as my mentor and the Bible as my playbook.

When I look back on it, I think God *had* called me to preach, but not at seventeen. I wasn't ready. Yet God was faithful enough to protect me and keep a covenant over me even then. Sometimes we step ahead of God, but He's still faithful to us. Later we realize, "I shouldn't have done that, but God was still with me."

AVOID SIN

Do you not know that the unrighteous will not inherit the
kingdom of God? Do not be deceived. Neither fornicators,
nor idolaters, nor adulterers, nor homosexuals, nor
sodomites, nor thieves, nor covetous, nor drunkards, nor
revilers, nor extortioners will inherit the kingdom of God.
1 Corinthians 6:9–10 NKJV

Maybe it's just your spouse or children doing something to
make you mad, but even in your own home you face temptation. Temptations will always surround us. Temptation itself
isn't a sin; acting upon the temptation is the sin. While we cannot avoid temptation, we can avoid sin.

And the temptations of pro football players? I've seen it all.
I've seen all kinds of women—from the ugliest to the prettiest—
chasing players. They can be very tempting.

Women pursue all athletes, but especially basketball players.
They'll camp out in the hotel, waiting on players to arrive.
They'll blatantly offer sex. They'll even ask players' wives to pass
along their invitations of sex, because they think the wives
won't care—and some of them don't. They just want the athletes for their money and bodies and glamour.

These women are wicked, and guys have fallen right into
their wickedness. They follow players they know are married,

and they don't care. They're wicked, and they need to be exposed—just as exposed as the guys are. Because what they do is wrong. They destroy families.

I know guys who are happily married, have three or four beautiful kids, and then women chase them and seduce them and their marriages are destroyed. I know of a couple of black players who were messing around with white women, and the women's mothers approved because of who the men were. The mothers would not have approved if they were just ordinary black men. Their daughters helped destroy these men's families, and the mothers didn't even care.

The men are just as much at fault as the women, but neither cared about destroying families, about committing sins, and that's sad. And when the parents condone it, that's even sadder.

You can even look at the president. If he harassed Paula Jones, then he deserves whatever he gets. But I assure you of one thing: Paula Jones didn't file that lawsuit just so she could sue Bill Clinton. Paula Jones set herself up to get wealthy. If the president did as she alleged, he was wrong, but we need to start making some women accountable too.

Yet he's one of our leaders, and our leaders need to be more responsible. As the Bible says in Proverbs, if you fall into the way of the adulterers, you lack common sense (6:32). That's why our country's in the condition it is today—because some of our presidents haven't used common sense to govern.

The Bible commands us to stay pure, and it's important whether you're a politician or an athlete. When you go to night-clubs and strip joints, you're going to be tempted, and if you go to enough strip joints, I believe you're going to fall into sin sooner or later. You're going to meet all sorts of people who want your money or body or fame, and they'll tempt you with drugs and women and too-good-to-be-true investments. When your body and mind are clouded by women or drugs or money, you lose focus on your career and family.

I've seen marriages ruined, careers ruined. I've seen team

AVOID SIN

morale affected. I've seen guys who thought they could separate their wickedness from their careers, but sooner or later, either during or after their careers, it caught up with them. And if teammates see one guy cheating, they start doing it too.

Cheating is so common. Some players' wives didn't like Sara because they saw her going home with her husband, while their husbands were leaving with somebody else. They knew their husbands were cheating on them, but they stayed with the players because of their kids or because of the money; their prenuptial agreements would have cost them too much money.

Adultery is a sin and so is homosexuality. But when I point out that the Bible condemns homosexuality, the gay rights activists say I hate them. I don't. I don't hate the sinner; I hate the sin. I know guys in our locker room who are just as wicked as any gay man could ever be. One of my teammates bragged about having sex with a woman just after she confided that she had been molested. She was trying to reach out to deal with her pain, and he took advantage of her. That's just as bad as the sin of homosexuality.

Let's not be deceived. Sin is sin, no matter what you call it.

IF YOU SIN, REPENT AND SEEK FORGIVENESS

> If we say that we have fellowship with Him,
> and walk in darkness, we lie and do not practice the truth . . .
> If we say that we have no sin, we deceive ourselves,
> and the truth is not in us. If we confess our sins,
> He is faithful and just to forgive us . . .
> and to cleanse us.
> *1 John 1:6, 8–9* NKJV

When we were in Philadelphia, a Cy Young Award winner for the Phillies bragged to reporters about his Christianity—while he was having an extramarital affair with a newspaper photographer.

His teammates just winked. Cheating was accepted. You know why it's accepted? Because the people who are supposed to be mentoring them and leading them on the right path accept it. The problem with people who profess to be Christians and continue to sin is that their pastors, their leaders, and their mentors don't demand that they do what's right. You know what? The pastors don't mind if that Cy Young Award winner belongs to their church, and they wouldn't dare kick him out of the church, because of the money he could give in tithes and offerings.

But Jesus says that if you see your brother in sin, you go to him. If he doesn't repent, then you take one or two other believers with you. If he still doesn't repent, then you take him before the church. If he doesn't repent even then, you kick him out of the church. (See Matt. 18:15–17.)

You excommunicate the unrepentant sinner. You consider him a heathen, a pagan. You throw him out because, otherwise, he can become a cancer, and his sin can spread through the whole congregation, as 1 Corinthians 5:4–6 tells us.

If you don't expel him, you're telling him that his sin is all right. When you let him know that it's not all right, then you let other people in the congregation know that it's not all right, and you're keeping some accountability.

The Bible says Christians must be accountable to one another. In 1 Corinthians 5, Paul tells about a man who was having sex with his father's wife—his stepmother. Paul said to kick this man out of the church and give him over to Satan so that he may be saved when the day of the Lord comes. Because when he's given over to Satan, he will realize, "I'm tired of living this way. I've got to get my life right and come back to the body of Christ."

When I say things like this, I receive a lot of ridicule. But I don't mind as long as I can help people stay pure and move in the direction God wants them to move. I don't profess to be perfect; I've shared some of my sins with you already. I'm like the bumper sticker:

Christians Aren't Perfect. They're Just Forgiven.

I was forgiven because I repented and changed. God will forgive you if you repent and reform your life. You are not alone. If you read the Bible, you will no longer put the biblical heroes on pedestals. You will see they were human and made the same mistakes we did, maybe much worse.

But no one who seeks God's grace is denied it. The Bible is full of stories of small men who sinned but repented and became great. David, the king of Israel, slept with a married woman, Bathsheba, got her pregnant, sent her husband to the front lines of battle to die, and God was so angry that He caused David's son to die. But when David repented, he and Bathsheba had more children, including Solomon, the future king and wise ruler.

Abraham was a liar. Peter denied Christ three times. Zacchaeus was a tax collector who cheated people. Another cheat, Jacob, became Israel. Even the worst of us can change and become the father of a great nation.

When you get to heaven, you might be surprised at some of the people you see there—and they might be surprised to see you!

PART NINE

THE BOOK OF
OBSTACLES

PERSIST IN THE FACE OF
HARDSHIP AND SUFFERING

We also glory in tribulations, knowing that
tribulation produces perseverance; and perseverance,
character; and character, hope.
Romans 5:3–4 NKJV

My back started hurting in June 1997, and it's been hurting ever since. The doctors suggested resting it before the 1998 season, and even that didn't help. Might have made it worse, in fact.

I have a condition called spondylolisthesis, a disk problem that probably occurred in childhood and has slowly degenerated, exacerbated by slamming into masses of muscle and bone for two decades. My fifth lumbar vertebra has slipped out, and my back goes into spasms. Also, I've got arthritis in my neck and back.

For years my back would go into spasms and I'd lock up on one side, but it always loosened up within a few days. But last June, it spazzed up and never stopped. And not just when I played. A lot of times I'll wake up crooked. If I sit too long, it stiffens up. If I stand too long, it stiffens up. I can live with a stiff neck—I've had that for years—but a football player needs a limber back.

My back was so stiff, in fact, I couldn't do the flexibility exercises to stretch it out. I couldn't lift weights as much, couldn't ride the exercise bike as much, couldn't jog. Using a Stairmaster made it worse. So everything I usually did to stay in shape, to keep the physical edge over the opposition, I couldn't do. I lost my edge in strength and stamina. I lost the explosion in my hips.

And then I got pneumonia. It made 1997 the most frustrating season of my career. If it was not my least productive year, it was one of them. I had some good games, but knowing my back wouldn't allow me to do things I know I can do was extremely frustrating. It caused me to lose some concentration and focus.

I would lock up on the right side so bad, I'd have a hard time bending over. Sometimes I had a hard time getting out of bed. I almost felt that if I moved the wrong way, my back would break. Sitting and watching film and going over the game plan would stiffen my back up, and I'd leave the room walking like an old man. Standing in the walk-throughs it would stiffen up.

On Sundays I'd get it loose enough, get the adrenaline flowing enough, so that I could start. But without my normal stamina, I spent more time on the sideline, and every time I stood or sat down, my back tightened up. The longer the game went on, the worse the back got. By the next morning you would swear I was sixty, seventy, eighty years old, the way I was walking.

I was in such misery during our game with Indianapolis in November that I had to leave the game for good. Afterward I laid on the floor in the locker room, and I honestly thought I was through for the season.

I seriously thought about quitting. I barely practiced that week, but I played that Sunday against Dallas, though not particularly well. A lot of people said, "He's too old; his body's been beaten down." The thing is, I've seen younger guys have this type of back pain and they wouldn't play. I've seen them retire. So don't tell me I'm too old. It's just that my back was hurting, and I don't think that has a lot to do with my age.

People also said I couldn't dominate the way I used to, and they were right. But I still led the NFC champions with eleven sacks and still made the Pro Bowl for the twelfth straight year, a league record. And I'm proud of that, because the doctors told me that most guys with my back wouldn't have even been on the field, let alone played every game.

They've also told me no operation can heal my back, and that playing will only make it worse.

So why play? Why not take the money and walk away while I still could? Number one, I'm a competitor. I don't like watching. I couldn't imagine going through what our cornerback, Craig Newsome, did—sitting out the whole season and watching his team go to the Super Bowl without him.

Number two, I knew God had done miracles on me before. I knew He could do it again, so I did my best to bear the pain. His miracles kept me pushing. No matter how bad my back was hurting, I always trusted God, and I still trust Him. I'm going to endure the pain until He says, "Okay, Reggie, now I'll do it," because I know He *can* do it.

There has not been a miracle yet, but I still believe God is a miracle worker. It may take years for Him to heal me, but I trust that He will. He did give me one miracle last year: persistence. I continued to go. I didn't look at God and blame Him and ask "Why?" because I know He always has a reason.

The greatest blessings I've ever experienced are the hard times, the sufferings, the afflictions, the backstabbing, the backbiting, the slander. They have been the greatest times for me because they've built my character and taught me how to handle myself.

The Bible says in Hebrews 5:8 that through suffering, Jesus learned how to obey. During our hardships, Sara and I have learned obedience, learned to depend totally on God. Whether it's been a bad back, or a business failing, or friends cheating us and harming us, we've faced plenty of adversity. Everybody does. Even the most successful people in the world are not immune from problems; they simply do not let problems stop them. Even the most righteous suffer tests and afflictions; that's how God teaches them.

And if He never heals my back, He just doesn't. It still won't make me distrust Him. I'll take it as one more sign that it's time for His other plans for me. God has always been faithful to me, and I won't let one little thing cause me to question Him.

I trust God. I trust Him with my back, my body, and my life.

LEARN FROM DEFEAT

Whoever loves instruction loves knowledge,
But he who hates correction is stupid.
Proverbs 12:1 NKJV

Here's what you learn from defeat: it hurts so much, do everything you can to avoid it.

Losing has caused me to lose sleep. It's gotten me irritated. It's tormented me. And I hate that irritation, that torment, that frustration. I hate it so much that it makes me wake up the next morning wanting to work harder all week to win the next game. If losing doesn't motivate you to work harder and win more than you lose, then you're going to be a loser for the rest of your life.

Losing eats me up. I try not to take it out on Sara and the kids, but sometimes I go to sleep and dream that we won, and then I wake up and realize we lost. It's like losing teases me, torments me, even in the midst of sleep. Or I lose sleep sometimes because I'm so disappointed with how the team played or how I played. What I try to do is get up and say, "I'm not going to let this overcome me. I'm going to defeat this."

In 1996, when we lost three regular-season games but won the championship, I totally forgot about the three losses. But last year, when we lost three again and made it to the Super

Bowl again only to lose, it definitely hurt. I'm like Vince Lombardi. I don't want to be second place.

I would have rather not gone to the Super Bowl than to go there and lose. I've been there twice and I'm 1–1. Some people say, "Well, you were there." Makes no difference. We lost.

John Elway went four times before he finally got one. In some respects, I'm better off than John. Because I always said, "Man, if I could just win one, then I'll be complete." John probably feels it's better to go four times, but if I'm only going to win once, I'd rather go just once. I imagine John was thinking, *Man, if we lose, I've lost four Super Bowls as the starting quarterback.* I'm sure it was gratifying to him to finally win one.

I know it was gratifying to me to finally win one. I'd never won a championship on any level. I don't regret coming back in 1997, but if I had known we'd lose Super Bowl XXXII, I would have retired and gone out on top.

I don't want to downplay the Broncos' performance. Their offensive line played well, and Terrell Davis really beat us. But if we had played our game, we would have beat them. It was extremely disappointing and hard to take because we were a much better team than we played. If I had felt the Broncos were the dominant team, then I could have handled this loss a lot better. They came in more prepared than we were; I can't put my finger on why we weren't as ready as we should have been.

Maybe it would have been different if our other defensive end, Gabe Wilkins, had not been hurt in the first quarter. Add Gabe's absence to my bad back and Gilbert Brown's sore ankle, and three-fourths of our defensive line was either absent or hobbled by injuries. If we had been healthy, it could have been different.

But I don't want to make excuses. They executed, and Terrell Davis ran well. We knew going into the game that he was dangerous; we saw how hard and quick he hit the hole. Our concerns came to fruition: he ran for 157 yards and three touchdowns and was named Super Bowl MVP.

I've taken a lot of heat for getting just one tackle. Well, I took a lot of heat from people who really don't know much about the game and who didn't take into consideration that the ball was only run to my side two times. It was a smart game plan on Mike Shanahan's part. He ran away from me.

I can take the heat from a coach, I can take the heat from an ex-player, but it's hard to take the heat from a person who's never played the game. The coaches let us know we didn't play well, and we admit it. I'm not going to say I had a good game at all. Even if I had ten sacks and we lost, it wouldn't have been a good game.

But for every crucifixion, a resurrection awaits. As much as the loss hurts, I realize even the best football teams win maybe seven out of ten games. Baseball's best players average fewer than four hits in ten at bats. So you have to learn from your inevitable defeats and use them as motivators. We used the disappointment of the 1995 NFC title game as a springboard to winning the Super Bowl in the 1996 season, and we'll keep the lessons of Super Bowl XXXII to fuel us in 1998.

SATAN'S DEMONS TEST US; GOD'S LOVE STEELS US

> There is no fear in love; but perfect love casts
> out fear, because fear involves torment. But he
> who fears has not been made perfect in love.
> We love Him because He first loved us.
> *1 John 4:18–19 NKJV*

Yes, I believe in Satan, and yes, I have helped cast out demons.

I won't name the player, but football fans know his name, and some might know a little about his story. On the plane to the 1996 Pro Bowl in Hawaii, he was troubled by lost sleep, lost games, and marital discord, and he started acting erratically. A devout teammate gave him a book of Scriptures to comfort him, and by the time he got off the plane, he was blurting out "Jesus is God." His wife and teammate feared he might jump or fall off the balcony of his hotel room, and they asked the Vikings' Cris Carter and me if we could make sure someone was with him at all times.

Now, some people might not see it this way, but when we saw the way he was acting, we knew he was possessed by demons. Everyone who knew him thought he was acting strangely. You could tell something was wrong. He would turn his head and look at you sideways and twist the ring on his finger and just growl,

"Grrrrrrrrrrrrr." Coaches would ask him questions and he would just stand there, finger his ring, and not answer.

We ministered to him. We read Bible verses. We talked out his problems. He wanted to change his life, and shortly before midnight, we walked right past a group of players who were partying at the poolside bar, and, wearing T-shirts and shorts, we waded into the Pacific Ocean and baptized him in a five-minute ceremony.

But it seemed the more we worked with him, the worse he got. He screamed a vile obscenity at a player just because he got up to get a drink of water. The people in control wanted to send him home, and if they did, he probably would have been committed to a mental hospital. I convinced Mike Holmgren, who was coaching our NFC team, to let him stay in Hawaii and just not play in the game.

We prayed and cast out demons and he still got worse. I called my pastor and asked him, "How do I handle this?"

"Stop praying for him," he said.

"Why?"

"Because every time you cast out a demon, you're casting out the wrong one."

"What do you mean?" I asked him.

"You've got to deal with the strong man, which is perversion. Demons mask the strong man. As the Bible says, when the house is swept clean, demons go to and fro and when they don't find other demons, they come back with seven demons worse than themselves. You guys are actually making it worse for him because you're casting out the wrong one. He has to humble himself. He has to want to be delivered."

For three straight nights he barely slept, and his wife was really distraught and scared. So all three of us players spent a night in their room. I dreaded spending that night with my three hundred pounds dangling off a little loveseat. But it was one of the most peaceful nights I've had. The next morning we woke up and he was fine. It was like nothing had ever been wrong with him.

I said, "Man, what was wrong?"

"It was almost like the last two days I was dreaming," he said.

I asked the Lord, "We didn't pray for him. We didn't cast out any demons. What happened?"

The Lord spoke to me and said, "It was the love you guys showed him that cast out the demons." The Bible says that perfect love casts out fear. That was a lesson for me. I realized then that for God to perform any miracles through us, or to heal anyone who's demonically oppressed, we must spend time with the afflicted person and show our love. To help anyone be delivered, we have to care. We showed our love and care, and with God's love, we cast out Satan's demons.

TOUGH TIMES
DO NOT LAST

For the Lord will not cast off forever.
Though He causes grief,
Yet He will show compassion
According to the multitude of His mercies.
For He does not afflict willingly,
Nor grieve the children of men.
Lamentations 3:31–33 NKJV

We see one kid blow another kid's head off.

We see drive-by shootings.

We see wars and diseases.

Every time bad things happen, we blame it on God.

But the thing is, we did that; God didn't. Man has brought these afflictions upon man because of our sin. We want to blame God for the hurt we inflict on one another, but a lot of this pain has nothing to do with God. Sometimes it doesn't even have much to do with the devil.

Flip Wilson used to get a laugh when he said, "The devil made me do it." But I don't think the devil can make us do anything. We choose whatever we want to do. We choose whether to do what's wrong or what's right. I wouldn't put it past man to have created diseases—and bad diseases—for the purpose of money and greed. Some cancers and diseases have come about because of cigarettes, smoking, pollution, and toxins. That's man. We have inflicted pain on one another.

All of us will have tough times in life. But tough times and suffering mature us and build character. God has to see if we're serious about wanting to serve Him, has to see if we can step forward in the midst of the hard times, has to see how much we love Him. All these tough times will pass if we endure to the end. And once we're with God, we don't have to worry about suffering anymore.

You might say, "Oh, that sounds great in theory, but I just lost a loved one, and he rarely did anything wrong. How can I even believe in a God who could so cruelly take away my loved one?"

You must keep the faith, even when you cannot see God in action. Faith is being sure of what you cannot see, as Hebrews 11 tells us. Sure, death hurts the survivors. I've mourned the loss of loved ones who died far too young. I have to realize that death is inevitable but heaven is available. What scares me is when the loved one doesn't know the Lord. If I know my late friend was a Christian, my pain can pass, but if I'm not sure, that hurts.

Jerome Brown and I played alongside each other with the Eagles. He was one of the game's best defensive tackles. He gave money to the community. He ran the Ku Klux Klan out of his hometown. He was an energetic, fun-loving man-child. He and his nephew, who planned to be a preacher when he grew up, died when Jerome drove too fast and rolled his Corvette on a rain-slicked road. Jerome was twenty-seven, his nephew just twelve. Jerome and I didn't hang out together, but I cared about him deeply. To see those two die that young was pretty hard to take.

It would have been much harder if Jerome's parents hadn't reacted the way they did. They lost a son and a grandson, but seeing these godly people at the funeral comforted me and a whole lot of other people. Because it was a celebration—

upbeat, full of music and dancing. It was sad that Jerome and his nephew died, obviously, but it was the most exciting funeral I've ever been to in my life.

If you know a person is going to the Lord, his funeral should be a celebration of his life and afterlife. Jerome's nephew knew God, but I don't know if Jerome did. He was wild and profane, but he was more kind, generous, and honest than a lot of churchgoers I know. So I have doubts but also hopes. The uncertainty is the hard part for me, even to this day. I think we celebrated for Jerome's nephew and in the hope that maybe Jerome had made a profession of faith we just didn't know about.

I know many people fear death, wondering what's in the next life and whether they will reach heaven. But I don't fear my own death because I know where I'm going. I don't fear the death of my children or my wife because I know where they're going.

I don't want a sad funeral. I want a choir. I want a celebration. Sure, my wife and my kids will be sad, but I want them to celebrate knowing I'm in a better place and I'm with the Father.

BE FLEXIBLE WHEN YOUR
GAME PLAN ISN'T WORKING

There are many plans in a man's heart,
Nevertheless the LORD's counsel—that will stand.
Proverbs 19:21 NKJV

As great as Brett Favre is, he doesn't end every possession with a touchdown. Sometimes his aim is off. Sometimes his receivers don't get open. Sometimes his protection breaks down and he has to heave the ball away or take a sack and punt. Sometimes the coaches spend all week working on the game plan only to discover it's just not working on Sunday, and they have to scrap it fast or lose.

Failure is inevitable in football, on offense, on defense, in little games, in big games. But it's no reason to panic. You just tinker and try, try, try again until you find what works.

Take Super Bowl XXXI, when we played New England. We were the favorites and jumped ahead, 10–0, and the game plan was working to perfection. But then Drew Bledsoe started figuring out our defense. On back-to-back series he drove the Patriots seventy-nine yards in six plays and fifty-seven yards in four more plays, and the Patriots led, 14–10. We had allowed an average of just thirteen points per game all season, and here we'd given up more than that and the first quarter wasn't even over. If we had fallen in love with our game plan and stubbornly refused to change, our dreams would have died.

But Fritz Shurmur hasn't been coordinating NFL defenses for a generation by accident. He's as cagey as they come. Just like that, Fritz changed our defense. We had been somewhat conservative, but we started blitzing more.

The knock on Bledsoe has always been that if you put pressure on him, he'll throw the ball up for grabs. So first we started sending our strong safety, LeRoy Butler, after him. Then we started blitzing one cornerback or the other, trying to keep Bledsoe guessing, confuse him, get him rattled. We changed our game plan, shook him up, and wound up with five sacks, four interceptions, and a 35–21 victory in football's ultimate game.

Do I need to describe the lesson? You can draw up what looks like the world's greatest game plan on paper, but if it isn't working on the field, you'd better change. If we hadn't changed, we would not have won Super Bowl XXXI.

You need the same flexibility in your game plan for life. If anything has helped teach me the importance of change, it's my marriage, even more than football. When I got married, I learned that if we wanted to stay together, I had to change. I changed then—and I'm still changing now.

And throughout my lifetime, I've realized that if I want to get closer to God, I've got to change. I've got to get rid of selfish motivations. I've got to stop thinking about myself and think about other people.

God has His own game plan. He wants us to devote ourselves to Him, wants us to be stewards of all creation. Are you following His game plan? Look at Mary and Joseph. They followed the game plan, even though it seemed vague and a little crazy, a virgin giving birth in a manger.

Look at Jonah. He did not follow God's game plan at first. The Lord told him to go to Nineveh and warn the people to change their wicked ways. But Jonah, like his nation of Israel,

BE FLEXIBLE WHEN YOUR GAME PLAN ISN'T WORKING

was arrogant. He thought God only cared about His people in Israel, and Jonah didn't want to travel more than five hundred miles to preach to the Gentiles in Assyria. What player wants to get traded to a lousy team? What professional wants to uproot his family for a job transfer to a wicked city?

And Nineveh was wicked in the extreme. Its army was famous for its cruelty, beheading or burning captured enemy soldiers. The Assyrian kings stacked up the dead like firewood in front of the gates of a conquered city. And they plundered the people, piling up the loot for their royal treasury; Nineveh was filled with the spoils of war from many nations. Jonah would have been crazy not to be a little afraid of going to Nineveh.

So Jonah fled from God, boarding a ship sailing in the opposite direction, and God so tossed that ship about, everyone feared it would capsize. Jonah told the sailors he had disobeyed God and if they threw him overboard, the storm would stop and they would be saved. They did as he said, and the storm died.

But Jonah didn't die. God sent a great fish to swallow him, and after Jonah prayed and repented for three days and vowed to go to Nineveh, God commanded the fish to spit Jonah out on dry land. Jonah journeyed to Nineveh, warned the people that God would destroy their city in forty days, and they fasted, donned sackcloth, sat in the dust, and prayed to God. And God saw that Jonah and Nineveh had changed, and showed His mercy.

Like Jonah, I did not quite understand why God called me to leave Philadelphia and my inner-city ministry for Green Bay, which lacked an inner-city ghetto and a winning team. But I have found my calling in the entire state. These people have taken to me like no other place I have called home, and I will live in Wisconsin even when I retire from football.

And have you noticed any critics calling the Packers losers anymore?

BE DOGGED AND RELENTLESS IN PURSUING YOUR DREAMS

> Those who wait on the LORD
> Shall renew their strength;
> They shall mount up with wings like eagles,
> They shall run and not be weary,
> They shall walk and not faint.
> *Isaiah 40:31 NKJV*

Let me take you back to Super Bowl XXXI again.

We went into the locker room feeling pretty good about the 27–14 lead we had taken just before half time. But when we came out for the second half, we found a haze of smoke and fumes on the floor of the Superdome. Every year the NFL tries to put on the biggest, gaudiest half-time show on earth, and maybe the fans liked it, but inside the dome, the residue from the pyrotechnics and Harley Davidsons couldn't escape, and the air felt hot and heavy. By the middle of the third quarter, a bunch of us were breathing hard, feeling really tired.

When I looked at the films later, I didn't look weak, but that's how I felt in the third quarter. I went to the sideline and told Fritz Shurmur and my position coach, Larry Brooks, "Man, I'm getting tired. I don't feel like my legs are there." They told me I was playing well and just to hang in there. I played a few more snaps and then went back to the sideline and told them,

"I'm really tired. I think I'd better come out." And again they encouraged me rather than let me quit.

But finally I took a blow for a couple of plays, and on the play I came back, Curtis Martin burst eighteen yards up the middle for a touchdown. I went to the sidelines and grabbed Eugene Robinson, our veteran free safety. "Man, I am not feeling good," I told him. "My legs are not under me. I'm not doing things I know I can do. You've got to pray for me or do something."

So right there on the sideline, Eugene quoted Isaiah 40:31 to me. And then he told me, "Just trust God. He'll be with you out there."

I'd like to say I felt a sudden surge of strength and adrenaline, but I didn't. I watched the Patriots kick the extra point to pull within 27–21, and I was worried. All my life I had pursued my vision of winning the Super Bowl, and I didn't want to get this close and lose my legs and my last chance.

But then came one of the most incredible sights I have ever witnessed: a record-breaking play by Desmond Howard. Two other teams had given up on Desmond, and when he had been hurt during our training camp, he was afraid he'd be released again, so we prayed together. Desmond barely beat out one of our veteran receivers for the last job, but he went on to set the league record for punt return yards. He returned three punts for touchdowns in the regular season and another in the playoffs, and already on Super Bowl Sunday, he had had some big returns.

Bill Parcells had warned his Patriots all week about Dangerous D, but here they kicked to him again. Desmond grabbed the ball at the one, burst up the middle toward the wedge, veered left behind a blocker, then juked out the kicker for the longest kick return in Super Bowl history. Brett threw a two-point conversion to Mark Chmura, and we were up 35–21; the whole complexion of the game changed.

When our defense went back on the field, the crowd was

jumping and our adrenaline was flowing. On the first play, the Patriots right tackle, Max Lane, dived at my legs to try to cut-block me. I jumped right over him and got to Bledsoe just after he unloaded a little dink pass. Even though the pass was complete, I was pumped. "Okay! I've gotten the power back in my legs!" I told myself.

On the next play, I drove inside on Max, used the club move I stole from Howie Long to lift him out of the way, and sacked Bledsoe. Now it was third and thirteen, and Max probably figured I'd go back to the club move. So he set up inside—and I went outside, flung him aside with my rip move, and sacked Bledsoe for the second play in a row.

The transformation since Eugene had quoted Isaiah 40:31 was amazing. "I'm rolling now!" I told myself. "I feel better than I have all game!"

The Patriots got the ball five times after Eugene quoted Scripture to me, and we forced two interceptions, three punts, and four sacks. I got three of those sacks, the last with less than two minutes left and our celebration already beginning.

The change in me was no coincidence. I know God gave me the strength. I credit God first, but I credit Eugene for being wise enough to quote that Scripture to me. I told him after the game, "Man, when you quoted that Scripture, that's what got me going."

His wisdom lifted me up. I had thought of that verse about "mounting up with wings like eagles" when I played for the Philadelphia Eagles, but I had never applied it. A lot of times you can quote Scripture verses, but they never apply until God is ready to reveal Himself to you. I believe God revealed His power and strength that day. To me. And to the whole world.

PART TEN

THE BOOK
OF FAITH

BELIEVE IN GOD

> Now faith is being sure of what we hope for and
> certain of what we do not see . . . And without faith
> it is impossible to please God, because anyone
> who comes to him must believe that he exists and
> that he rewards those who earnestly seek him.
> *Hebrews 11:1, 6 NIV*

I was saved at thirteen and licensed as a minister at seventeen, but not until I was thirty-five did I learn what true faith was all about.

My revelation came after we beat the Minnesota Vikings to conclude the 1996 regular season. We had home-field advantage throughout the playoffs, and a lot of people were picking us to win the Super Bowl. I had never won a championship, but I had craved one so desperately for so long, I had come to believe I would end my career without one.

This is when God spoke to me. He asked me, "Why do you think I'm finally giving you a chance to win the Super Bowl?"

"I don't know," I said. "I know it's not because of my faith."

God said, "You're exactly right. It's not because of your faith, because your definition of faith is wrong."

I said, "What do you mean?" and I started to think. My idea of faith was if I believed in God, that would give me eternal life.

Or if I got down on my knees and asked God to do something for me and believed in my heart that it would happen, He would give it to me. If I stepped on the field believing we would beat a team and we ended up losing, I always wondered, "I know I had faith. What happened?" My definition of faith was really shallow.

God told me to read Hebrews 11. It starts off saying faith is the substance of things hoped for. I had always hoped for a championship. The second part of verse one talks about the evidence of things not seen. When I read the rest of Hebrews 11, I realized that not one of those heroes of the faith asked God to give him or her something. Instead, they are said to have had faith because they believed God, followed God, and obeyed God.

And I realized something I'd never seen before: that people aren't credited with faith because they believe something will happen; they are credited with faith because they believe what God tells them to do and they do it. God does not reward your desire; He rewards your obedience.

So faith is really obedience. If you look up the words in Greek, they practically mean the same thing. I looked up a few more words: *faith, faithfulness, confidence, trust, belief.* They all go back to obedience. When you read those words in the Bible, you can replace them with the word *obedience.*

Many Christians today have been bamboozled. They've been taught the wrong definition of faith. Faith is trusting what the eye cannot see. Just as a little boy trusts his father to catch him when he jumps, we must make the leap of faith and trust our Father, whom the eye cannot see. Faith is more than believing in God and thus expecting Him to answer your prayers. Faith is believing God, *and* following God, *and* obeying God. When He tells us to do something and we move on His word, that is faith.

God told me, "I have brought you this close to the championship not because you desired it or because you asked me for it, but because you obeyed Me. When human wisdom told you to go to San Francisco, you heard Me telling you to go to Green Bay. You took a lot of flak for that decision. You were misunderstood and criticized. But you trusted Me, you went—and I counted that obedience toward your faith."

That realization has revolutionized my life. And so on January 26, 1997, when I set a Super Bowl sack record and the Green Bay Packers won the trophy named after their late, great coach, Vince Lombardi, I went on television and told millions of viewers around the world, "I want to say, 'Thank you, Jesus.'"

TRUST IN GOD AND YOU CAN BELIEVE IN YOURSELF

Do not be afraid of sudden terror,
Nor of trouble from the wicked when it comes;
For the LORD will be your confidence,
And will keep your foot from being caught.
Proverbs 3:25–26 NKJV

We were driving toward the Dead Sea when we came across a poor Arab shepherd. We tried to give him water, but he wouldn't take our water. Then we tried to give him shekels, but he wouldn't take our money. Then my next-door neighbor Todd noticed the holes in the man's tennis shoes, so Todd took his sneakers right off his own feet and offered them to the shepherd. When he tried them on, you could see the glow in his face. He threw away his shoes, and he was so excited, he ended up taking our shekels too. But he seemed more proud of the shoes than anything.

Todd walked barefoot back to the tour bus. It was a blessing to see how giving he was, to see how happy he made that poor shepherd. Todd didn't want the television cameramen who accompanied us to film it or build him up. He was embarrassed because he hadn't done it for attention or glory, but out of the goodness of his heart. But sometimes God compliments you through other people to let you know He's proud of you, that He appreciates what you are doing for Him.

When people compliment me, I usually say something like, "It wasn't me, it was God working through me." I don't want people to think it's false humility. I give God the honor and glory both in my heart and my public professions. As Todd did with the shepherd, I strive for humility instead of arrogance.

Why? Because we have too much arrogance in this country. We have CEOs who think they're the only ones who built their corporations. They think, "I'm The Man. I should make millions and forget about the workers." There's arrogance in our politicians in Washington, D.C. There's arrogance in my profession—and in basketball, baseball, and hockey too—because guys who came from unenviable backgrounds are making it big now, patting themselves on the back, and saying they've made it. Wealthy men buy the teams, which gives them a sense of power, and they become extremely arrogant.

But whether they are the president of the United States or the president of a corporation, these men should realize their money and power cannot buy their way into heaven nor buy their way out of hell. Those arrogant, prideful men think more of themselves than they should.

Now, don't get me wrong. It's important to believe in yourself. The old saying is true: whether you believe you can or believe you can't, you're right. But I think arrogant people miss an important point. I figure the best way to believe in yourself is by first trusting God and allowing Him to do His work in you. If God is in you, you gain self-confidence. Because once we trust God, we have no insecurities. We won't worry about critics' opinions because we trust totally in God's opinion about who we are. We won't base our sense of worth on people's opinions or material wealth because when Jesus died for our sins, we were given sacred worth.

If I base my self-worth on my career, what do I do when I'm retired and no longer "Reggie White, all-time sack leader"? If I base my self-esteem on my money, how can I ever be satisfied unless I'm Bill Gates?

I'm thirty-six years old and I still have people, even ministers, tell me, "This is what God wants you to do." How do they know what God wants for me? They're not God. If I let them, they would make me insecure and dependent on them, when God is letting me know, "The only people you need are Me and the people I provide to help you." That gives me self-confidence, because I trust God and what He's doing in my life.

If you read the Bible, you'll see you are to lean toward belief in Christ before belief in self. Many Scriptures warn against false self-esteem. Pride goes before a fall (Prov. 16:18). Blessed are the poor in spirit (Matt. 5:3). The Lord detests all the proud of heart; they will not go unpunished (Prov. 16:5).

So show an attitude of gratitude by staying humble. Realize that nothing you've attained has come on your own, that God has blessed you. God did not allow me to be a football player because of how good I was. He allowed me to play this game because of His grace, because He knew I would lift up His name. I'm grateful God gave me the opportunity to play this game, and I'm even more grateful He gave me the opportunity to use my time and resources to help others.

Trust God and be confident in the abilities He gave you. Let God be the source of your strength and courage. You'll give up on yourself before God will. Trust Him to fight for you, but also realize your role in reaching your goals.

Before we played Carolina for the 1996 NFC championship, Mike Holmgren told me, "You've waited your whole life for this game. You've been talking about it for years. Now it's really gonna happen. So make sure you focus all your energy on it. Go out and do all the things you've been promising. This team looks to you for leadership and emotion. If they see it in you, they'll find it in themselves."

"I know," I replied. "I'll be there. Count on it."

PART ELEVEN

THE BOOK
OF LOVE

SHOW YOUR LOVE

Love is patient, love is kind. It does not envy, it does not
boast, it is not proud. It is not rude, it is not self-seeking, it
is not easily angered, it keeps no record of wrongs. Love
does not delight in evil but rejoices with the truth. It always
protects, always trusts, always hopes, always perseveres.
Love never fails.
1 Corinthians 13:4–8 NIV

As Americans, we're taught to misunderstand love. We're
taught to focus on sexual love. In magazines and movies, in
soap operas and advertisements, we're deluged with sex. Sex
sells. Sex is big business. But sex is just a small part of love.

The Greek language defines several types of love. One is
phileo, which refers to filial love or brotherly love. That's where
the word *Philadelphia* comes from. The Bible uses *phileo* to
describe the close bonds of relationship with family and
friends. Then there's *eros,* or sexual love. That love can be fulfilled within marriage, but it should not be the main part of
love in the marriage.

The main part should be *agape* love, which is unconditional,
the same love God has for humankind. Agape love is not selfish
or sexual. If you get up in the morning and your breath smells

and your hair looks bad, your partner has to look at your heart and overlook your appearance.

Every day on TV you hear people say, "I love you." They're actors. They don't mean it. We have many men and women telling their spouses and children they love them, but they don't show it. They might as well be actors on TV.

Agape love is shown by actions. It's easy to tell my wife and kids I love them, but if I'm not doing things to prove it, it's not true love.

How do you show love? Follow the advice of 1 Corinthians 13. Praise the people you love. Build their self-esteem. Apologize if you've wronged them. Do things with them. Go out to dinner and go on vacation with them. Talk with them. Listen to them.

Sometimes Sara will tell a story for fifteen minutes instead of just getting to the point in two minutes. I have to be willing to sit and listen the whole fifteen minutes. If we communicate, we express our love. If I get her flowers, I'm expressing my love. And I'm not talking about the flowers that are almost expected on holidays or special occasions. I'm talking about surprising my wife with flowers just to show my affection.

A woman wants to be made love to more out of bed than in bed. Having sex with your wife does not prove you love her. Love is doing the little things. If she wants you to pick your shoes off the floor, do it. If she wants you to go somewhere with her, do it. If she wants you to wash the dishes or clean up when you don't normally do it, do it this time.

I've told men, "If you do special things for your wife, when you want to make love, she won't have a problem with it, because you've already expressed your love." A woman does not want to be a pawn used by a man to fulfill his sexual needs. She wants her needs fulfilled by the things you do for her and the way you romance her. You don't stop wooing her once the dates and engagement and wedding are over. The romancing has just begun . . .

FIND A MODEL SPOUSE

Who can find a virtuous wife?
For her worth is far above rubies.
The heart of her husband safely trusts her;
So he will have no lack of gain.
She does him good and not evil
All the days of her life.
Proverbs 31:10–12 NKJV

The Bible defines the perfect wife in Proverbs 31, and if you ask me, Sara is a Proverbs 31 wife.

Let me recite the verses and explain how I believe Sara fulfills each one. And as you read, if you're married or looking to get married, maybe you can contemplate how you and your partner are doing.

"Who can find a virtuous wife? / For her worth is far above rubies" (v. 10 NKJV). Well, Sara's price to me is far beyond rubies. She's worth more to me than riches.

"The heart of her husband safely trusts her" (v. 11 NKJV). I trust Sara with all my heart.

"She does him good and not evil / All the days of her life" (v. 12 NKJV). I don't believe Sara is going to rob me or diminish me or try to take my position away.

"She seeks wool and flax / And willingly works with her

hands. / She is like the merchant ships, / She brings her food from afar. She also rises while it is yet night / And provides food for her household / And a portion for her maidservants. / She considers a field and buys it; / From her profits she plants a vineyard" (vv. 13–16 NKJV). Sara handles all our business. She handles our taxes. She has a business mind; I don't. I let her handle our business and she saves me tons of money.

I could have told Sara, "You submit to me. Leave the money alone. This is what I'm going to do and this is what you're going to do and that's the way it's going to be." But marriage is a partnership. She's been given gifts and I've been given gifts, and I have to allow her to pursue her gifts as she allows me to follow mine.

"She girds herself with strength / And strengthens her arms" (v. 17 NKJV). Sara works out and keeps herself in great shape.

"She perceives that her merchandise is good, / And her lamp does not go out by night" (v. 18 NKJV). Sara stays up late into the night making sure our business is handled right and that things don't get out of whack. She's doing a lot to make sure that things stand corrected in this house.

"Yes, she reaches out her hands to the needy" (v. 20 NKJV). When Sara and I got married, Sara did not want to give money away. I was a giver. If somebody needed a house, I'd give it to him. Sara taught me how to give wisely, and I taught her how to give generously.

Instead of just giving without responsibility, she taught me how to give—to listen to God and know whom to give to and what to give to. I get letters now from people thanking us for our donations for their ministries or food banks or charities, and I know I didn't give it, Sara did. I take pleasure in knowing that she's giving also. We've taught each other. We've helped each other in our weaknesses.

HUSBANDS, LEAD AND SERVE YOUR WIVES

Wives, submit to your husbands as to the Lord.
For the husband is the head of the wife as Christ is
the head of the church, his body, of which he is Savior.
Now as the church submits to Christ, so also wives
should submit to their husbands in everything.
Husbands, love your wives, just as Christ loved the
church and gave himself up for her.
Ephesians 5:22–25 NIV

Many women have problems with the notion they must submit to their husbands. The issue caused a firestorm after the 1998 Southern Baptist convention. But this is biblical. This is what the great apostle Paul says wives must do in his letter to the Ephesians. The man is the one who should control the family, who should have the final say-so.

I'm not talking about dictators demanding their women clean house and have babies and not have any responsibility or independence. I'm talking about a partnership. I'm talking about sitting down and discussing the issues and trying to agree. If we don't agree, I have the final say. If I prove to be wrong, I have to be man enough to apologize. If I prove to be right, I'm not going to come and rub it in her face and say, "I told you."

Sara is my friend, my best friend. I'm not going to treat my best friend as though she's less than I am. I'm going to treat my best friend as if she's on the same level. Many times she has advised me not to do something and much later I realized, "Thank God I didn't do it." Other times I realized, "If only I had listened to her, I could have saved a whole lot of money." But if God speaks to me and says, "It's time to move," then no matter what she tells me or anybody else tells me, we have to move. She knows that when God speaks, we have to move.

Ladies, before you fling this book across the room wishing you could whomp me over the head with it, let me explain. I will admit that most men in this country have been wimps and chumps. They have not learned how to love and lead their wives. If I love my wife and I care for her and treat her like she wants to be treated, then she's going to be honored and not demeaned even when she submits. I believe—and I was taught this by my pastors, Brett and Cynthia Fuller and Jerry Upton—that a woman submitting to her husband depends on how well he treats her.

I tell people this is my motto: if I treat my wife like the queen she is, she'll treat me like the king I am.

To understand the concept fully, it's important you don't skim over Ephesians. Read each part carefully. Ephesians says my wife should submit herself to me as to the Lord. Submit not to Reggie, but to God. Not that I'm God, but I'm supposed to comfort and protect her.

Then it says the husband is the head of the wife as Christ is the head of the church. So I'm looking out for her well-being just as Christ was looking out for the well-being of the church. Then it says wives are subject to their husbands as the church was subject to Christ. Sara is subject only to me, not to any other man.

What men don't realize is that when Paul says we should love our wives, he says something even stronger: just as Christ loved the church and gave Himself for her. Christ served the church. In Scripture Jesus says that the "greatest among you shall be your servant" (Matt. 23:11 NKJV). He didn't come so His disciples could serve Him; He came to serve His disciples.

What this means is that, as husbands, we must serve our wives and our children. We didn't marry our wives so they could serve us. We married them so we could serve them. That's what Paul says: Husbands, love your wives even as Christ loved the church and gave Himself for her. Ephesians says if you do this, you'll make her holy and without blemish.

Finally, Ephesians 5:28 says husbands ought to love their wives as their own bodies, because he who loves his wife loves himself. If a man constantly cheats on his wife, or lies to her, or abuses her physically or verbally, he really doesn't love himself. And when a man doesn't love himself, he will not love his wife or anyone else who's around him.

Listen, I know marriage isn't always easy. There were times early in our marriage that Sara and I thought about breaking up, but I don't think we seriously contemplated it because we were too scared of God. I often wondered if I wanted to stay locked up and tied down. Brett and Cynthia and Jerry mediated our disagreements, our personality conflicts, because sometimes it's easier to accept an objective outsider telling you you're wrong.

I think Jerry gave us the best advice. He said we should treat our marriage as though we could get a divorce at any time, because then we wouldn't get complacent. The Bible says in 1 Corinthians 10:12, "Let him who thinks he stands take heed lest he fall" (NKJV).

When I first married Sara, I used to ask God when He was going to change her. I read Edwin Louis Cole's book, *Maximized Manhood,* and he asked the same question: "God, when are you going to change my wife?"

And the Lord said, "It ain't her. It's you."

Reading that passage hit me like a ton of bricks. I realized that if I wanted Sara to act right, I needed to straighten up. I needed to serve her instead of expecting her to serve me. I realized this relationship was not a dictatorship but a partnership. The Bible says I'm over my wife, but I shouldn't lord over her like a general or admiral. We're partners.

LOVE AND LEAD YOUR FAMILY

And you, fathers, do not provoke your children to wrath,
but bring them up in the training and
admonition of the Lord.
Ephesians 6:4 NKJV

Most of Jeremy's soccer games are played on Saturday afternoons, and I used to miss them. I'd get home around noon, and after practicing all week I'd be extremely tired. So I would try to conserve my energy for my game the next day.

But I went to a soccer game last season, and afterward, as Jeremy and I were walking off the field, he looked up at me. Something in his eyes said, "I'm glad you're here. Thanks for coming."

It was a look that broke my heart. Because it was a look of appreciation—an appreciation for the love I showed by attending that one game. I got back to my truck and almost started crying.

I realized then, *If I could have only gone to these games when he was younger.* Now I want to make up for the times I wasn't there for him.

So I go to his basketball games too. He's not the greatest player, but he's still a kid, he's learning, and I can tell he appreciates my being there. I can tell Jecolia appreciates it when I go to some of her singing recitals. Every time I go, the first thing she does is come and hug me.

I look back and say, "Man, I was missing out on this."

I don't want to miss out anymore.

I want to be a hero for my kids. I want to be there for them. I want them to have the same experiences Sara and I do. I took them out of school in March so they could visit Israel with us, because I wanted them to see how different cultures are, wanted them to interact with different people, wanted them to see where Christianity started. Because someday Jeremy and Jecolia will have to carry on the ministry Sara and I have established.

I try to allow them to be as much a part of the grownups' conversations as possible, to let them know their opinions do matter. Jeremy can talk so much that I must admit that sometimes I just sit and say, 'Mmmm hmmmm, uh huh, okay," and not really know what he's saying. I want him to at least *think* he has my attention.

But if I find myself getting annoyed and thinking I don't have time for him, I snap out of it when I remember the things I never got from a man. I probably go overboard trying to be the dad I never had. Often, I get envious of my kids because I wish I'd had a dad to talk to me about the same things we talk about now. I want them to feel they can talk to me. I want them to feel their parents are their best friends. I don't want them to go to a counselor or a friend to share their problems. I want them to share with their mom and dad, knowing we love them and care about them more than anyone else could, knowing we will understand and won't beat them down for their mistakes.

I want to lead them and serve them just as I do my wife. The only way I can inspire Sara and my children is by being the ultimate team leader. I have to get my point over so we can win. Sometimes I come across in a stern way, but most of the time in a loving way.

I know this: I can't and won't trade them for anything in this world. No matter how mad Sara and I get with each other, we've got to work it out, because of our love for each other and our children.

My kids bless me all the time. They've been honor students throughout school. Jeremy is in seventh grade, Jecolia in fifth grade. They have a true dedication to what they're doing and to their parents.

Jecolia writes us little notes to let us know how much she loves us. Jecolia and Jeremy buy me hats that say, "I love my dad." They have bought me a comic strip about fatherhood, a shirt that tells what a father is, and a dad ring.

These things aren't corny, they're mementos of love. I cherish them.

I keep that dad ring in our jewelry box.

By my bed.

Close to my heart.

DISCIPLINE YOUR CHILDREN

Train up a child in the way he should go,
And when he is old he will not depart from it.
Proverbs 22:6 NKJV

I believe in whuppings.

And I don't mean just a little love tap on the behind. I mean a good *thwappp!* with a belt.

The number is based on the severity of what they did wrong, but I give no more than five licks. When you whup your kids with more than five or six licks, you're angry. I don't discipline them out of anger; I discipline them out of duty. Because discipline isn't about punishing, it's about training, correcting, and molding.

We all need discipline. Proverbs 3:11–12 (NIV) tells us, "My son, do not despise the LORD's discipline / and do not resent his rebuke, / because the LORD disciplines those he loves, / as a father the son he delights in." So the Bible teaches me that not only must I expect God to discipline me, I must discipline my children. And it tells me discipline is a *good* thing.

Discipline doesn't necessarily mean corporal punishment; a whupping is just one version of discipline. I'd rather use the sternness in my voice than the sternness in my belt.

I can honestly say over the thirteen years we've been

married and the twelve years we've had children, that's what we've done. We've talked more than we've whupped. I will whup them for lying or hurting each other. I've often told them, "If one of you punches so hard that the other starts crying, both of you are getting the whupping because you got rough with each other."

If their offense is not serious, I'll give them one or two licks, but one or two they'll remember. After that, I'll talk to them and ask them to explain why I punished them. Once they explain why I did it, I hug them and kiss them. I want them to know I might not love their actions, but I'll always love them. Because I think parents damage children when they discipline them but don't say why. I don't want to leave my children. I don't want to abuse them. I want to teach them.

And I think they've learned. My kids haven't gotten a single whupping in the past two years, but they do remember the last one they got.

Some people claim spanking with your hand, let alone a belt, is child abuse. I think that's nonsense. I'll agree, it's abuse if you don't explain why you did it, if you don't show your love. But I think you abuse your children when you *don't* discipline them. Because you *have* to teach your children, and sometimes teaching requires negative reinforcement. They must suffer the consequences if they disobey, or they'll grow up to be wild, unruly, uncaring children and adults.

Lack of discipline has led to a lot of our country's problems today. All these so-called experts said punishing children would ruin their self-esteem, and permissive parents stopped disciplining their kids, and look at the problems we're having now. Kids who don't respect authority. Kids who don't know and don't care about what's right and what's wrong. Kids killing kids. Kids having kids. Kids drinking booze and smoking cigarettes and doing drugs.

We've allowed the government to tell us how to raise our children, and I cannot allow the government to discipline my kids. I follow advice straight from the Bible. Proverbs 13:24 says, "He who spares his rod hates his son, / But he who loves him disciplines him promptly" (NKJV). Just as a shepherd uses a rod to discipline his sheep, we must use the same reinforcement with our children. I want to teach them respect. I don't want them to be rude. I want them to call adults Mr. or Mrs. and say "Yes, sir" and "Yes, ma'am." The Bible says if we train them well, they won't depart from it when they get older. So we communicate and share the word of God with them, work with them in school, and discipline them.

The Bible says I can't spare the discipline.

Because the results last an eternity.

Because my kids deserve what I didn't get from my father.

Discipline.

And love.

I don't just tell my kids I love them. I show them. I try to make sure I kiss and hug Jecolia and Jeremy as much as possible every day. As a father, it's easy to hug and kiss your daughter. But a survey taken a few years ago said that sixty to seventy percent of fathers don't hug and kiss their sons after the age of six. A lot of boys don't want to be kissed in public by their parents, but I tell Jeremy, "If I kiss you and you scream like a girl, I'll give you a lick." And I slobber all up and down his face.

So Jeremy accepts a public kiss from his dad. It beats the alternative.

PART TWELVE

THE BOOK OF
FULFILLMENT

SEEK SERENITY

Come to me, all you who are weary and burdened,
and I will give you rest. Take my yoke upon you
and learn from me, for I am gentle and humble
in heart, and you will find rest for your souls.
For my yoke is easy and my burden is light.
Matthew 11:28–30 NIV

When I was a kid, I would sit under a tree in the woods and just look around and enjoy the beauty of nature, and it was so relaxing, I'd fall fast asleep. Even today I like to sit out at night when it's warm and quiet and just listen to the leaves blowing in the wind. The serenity soothes and comforts me and alleviates stress.

We need that sometimes. Sitting outside and admiring the work God has done is a great way to communicate with Him. The book of Romans says it's evident that God is real by what we see around us, from the sky to the trees to the birds to the blowing of the wind to the waving of grass (1:19–20).

As a kid I would go out on the porch and watch the lightning and listen to the thunder. At times it would be scary, but mostly it excited me. A smooth rain beating on the windows and roof calmed me. The same thing works for Jeremy now; he listens to a little sound machine that plays ocean waves and tropical rains.

Those sounds don't work for me anymore. I don't know why. Maybe it's because as adults we get so wrapped up in our jobs and day-to-day obligations that we don't slow down long enough to enjoy God's nature show. We don't take time to listen to the dripping rain or the rustling leaves.

But we need to balance career, family, and faith. We need to satisfy our mental, physical, social, and spiritual selves. We need to examine if our daily routine is in harmony with our goals, or if we've fallen into a rut we cannot escape. We need more than a fat paycheck and a manicured lawn and a shiny car. We need to take the blinders off our souls and discover the serenity that nature used to bring us.

Let the lawn and the laundry go every once in a while and revert to a carefree naiveté. Fly a kite. Take a hike. Ride a pony. Hurl yourself down a scary slide and splash in the water. Ride a roller coaster and scream your fool head off. Let down your guard. Lift up your spirit. Gaze at the stars, the moon, the mountains, the oceans. Stop and pick a wildflower.

I'm reminded of a little girl and her "art." She spends hours drawing pictures, cutting and pasting paper together, writing, "I LUV U, MOMME." The spelling is wrong. The letters are misformed, all out of proportion, traversing the page like a drunk trying to walk a straight line. The coloring is outside the lines. The art is primitive, not pretty, and she makes piles of it that she scatters all over the house. And we carp at the crayon marks on the wall and the paper scraps on the floor. No. Treasure it. While you can.

Every once in a while, turn off the cordless phone and the cell phone and the beeper and e-mail and voice mail. Escape. Ban newspapers and TV newscasts. Forget the worries about the stock market, the killings, the drug lords. *Carpe diem.* Seize the day. You never know. It might be your last. And wouldn't it be a shame if you spent it worrying for nothing? What are you waiting for? Tomorrow? As the great football philosopher

Walter Payton said of his long Super Bowl chase, "Tomorrow is never promised to anyone."

Go to the zoo and laugh at the monkeys. Go to the park and feed the ducks.

Go anywhere and feed your soul.

Seek harmony in your mind and music. I created a Christian record company to give people a sound they like. They mostly like secular music because some Christian music is extremely boring. But good Christian music feeds my soul and builds me up.

Music does soothe your soul. That's why David was brought to Saul—to play songs for him. Saul had been tormented by a demon, but the music soothed his soul. I've been to church services where the music was exactly what I needed. It got me up out of the chair and excited me more than the sermon did.

Talking with my wife, kids, and friends can feed my soul. Seeking God and what He wants in my life feeds my soul too. Sometimes I get the word while I'm praying. Other times I read a Bible study booklet. Sometimes I meditate. God just wants us to talk with Him. He doesn't care when. We don't need an appointment. We do need tranquility.

Scrap regrets about the past and worries about the future.

Celebrate life.

FIND FULFILLMENT

> Here is the conclusion of the matter:
> Fear God and keep his commandments,
> for this is the whole duty of man.
> *Ecclesiastes 12:13* NIV

T ravel back in time nearly three thousand years. Plop yourself down on the streets of Jerusalem and start talking to the men. They'll tell you that King Solomon has it all. David's son is Everyman's hero. Ooooh, boy, did he have it all!

He ruled the united kingdom of Israel for forty years, and never once had to run for election or compromise with Congress. He was the original renaissance man—about twenty-five hundred years before the Renaissance. He was the wisest man who ever lived. He was a judge with understanding "as measureless as the sand on the seashore" (1 Kings 4:29 NIV). He was such a master of nature and philosophy, men from all nations journeyed to hear him speak.

He was equal parts Hemingway, Hammerstein, and Hefner, writing three thousand proverbs and a thousand songs, and loving seven hundred wives and three hundred concubines.

And rich? He had more money than Bill Gates, Warren Buffett, and Fort Knox combined. He built a temple coated with gold and a royal palace with a throne of gold and ivory. He owned thousands of horses and sheep, all kinds of houses and gardens and parks, precious spices and stones and woods, and so much gold and silver, he "made silver as common in Jerusalem as stones" (1 Kings 10:27 NKJV).

But read Ecclesiastes, which is Greek for *teacher,* and you will see that the greatest teacher lamented all these achievements that we spend our lives striving for as "vanity and grasping for the wind" (1:14 NKJV). I love that imagery: the futility of trying to capture the wind in your bare hands.

Solomon found that the more knowledgeable he became, the more he learned about sorrow and grief. He found the sage and the fool met the same fate—death. He wrote that he sought pleasure and laughter, wine and folly, singers and lovers, and gave himself "whatever my eyes desired" (2:10 NKJV), yet found they were only fleeting pleasures.

He decided all labor and achievement sprang from man's envy of his neighbor, but the rich man died as surely as the poor man, the achiever as surely as the animal. Solomon discovered his work had been burdensome and his mind troubled, yet all that toil meant nothing when he died, because he couldn't take his riches to the grave. He found a man never content with his wealth, so busy working he had neither son nor brother nor enjoyment. He realized, "Whoever loves money never has money enough; / whoever loves wealth is never satisfied with his income. / This too is meaningless" (Eccl. 5:10 NIV).

He realized the wicked sometimes live longer than the righteous, that the race is not always to the swift or the battle to the strong, or wealth to the brilliant. Man doesn't control his success on earth; God does. And the only way to eternal life, to true fulfillment, is through God.

He concluded that we have but one duty in this life: trust God and obey His commandments.

After three thousand years, you would have thought the great philosopher's lesson would have sunk in by now. But here we are, vanity of vanities, still trying to grasp the wind. We grab after money and fame and significance, but when we achieve our goals, we often find ourselves strangely unexcited, and we ask the same questions as Solomon: Is that all there is? Why break our necks to live when we're only living to die?

Solomon realized you cannot find the meaning of life through life. He discovered he needed to know God before he could understand what life is all about, before he could stop fretting about dying because he knew God gave him eternal life.

Just as ancient men saw Solomon as having it all, I know some modern men see me the same way. And it's true that I've got a couple of houses, a fleet of cars, a slew of awards, and a bankful of money. But if I tried to measure myself against the most accomplished men in, say, wealth, I'd fall several zeroes short of Bill Gates. I don't measure myself that way. My success and happiness do not come from wisdom or wealth or accomplishment.

My fulfillment comes from the only thing that matters: I fear God and try to obey His commandments, and because I do, I have eternal life.

So I do have it all—and so can you.

You can't work for it. You can't earn it. You gain it not by your righteousness but simply by asking for God's mercy.

IS THAT ALL THERE IS?

Do not love the world or anything in the world. If anyone
loves the world, the love of the Father is not in him.
For everything in the world—the cravings of sinful man,
the lust of his eyes and the boasting of what he has and
does—comes not from the Father but from the world.
The world and its desires pass away, but the man
who does the will of God lives forever.
1 John 2:15–17 NIV

We won Super Bowl XXXI the night of January 26, 1997, and
the next morning we were supposed to go straight from New
Orleans to a parade through downtown Green Bay.

But on the plane ride home, two men on the Packers' board
of directors, John Underwood and Peter Platten, walked back to
the seat where I was napping and prodded me awake.

"Reggie," they said, "we need you to pray."

"For what?" I said, a tad groggy.

"There's a snowstorm in Green Bay, and we might have to
land in the Twin Cities. The pilot told us somebody needs to
start praying, or we're not landing in Green Bay."

And if we were forced to go to Minnesota, we would have
had to wait around and cancel the parade. Plus, I was supposed

to leave Tuesday for the Pro Bowl, and I thought, *Oh, no, how am I supposed to get to Hawaii?*

We prayed, and then I fell back to sleep.

I woke up about fifteen minutes later and walked up the aisle and found Peter and John. "The prayer's been answered. We're landing in Green Bay," they said.

"Praise God!" I said.

So God answered my prayers two days in a row, but you know what? When I achieved my lifelong dream, the fulfillment wasn't the fantasy I thought it would be. I was too exhausted to have any emotion. Exhausted not only from playing but from celebrating in New Orleans and then flying home and going through the parade and then getting the whole family packed and ready early the next morning to fly all day to Hawaii.

Having all the players and coaches ride in an open-air bus for over two hours in Green Bay, Wisconsin, in late January might not have been the greatest idea. I got lucky and rode in a warm fire truck, but everybody else was freezing! Don't get me wrong, it was all worth it, because the fans had been waiting out in the cold since about ten o'clock in the morning—and waiting to celebrate another Super Bowl victory after twenty-nine years.

But though it was an exciting day, it wasn't an extremely good day, because we were tired and dreading the long flight the next day. We didn't have a chance to sit back and enjoy the week and let the victory sink in.

In the midst of winning the big game, I had told the media my career was finally complete. But I forgot it wasn't over. It will never be complete as long as I have the opportunity to win another one. Maybe I'm wrong, maybe I'm greedy, but as long as I play this game, my goal always will be to win the big game. I realized that even more after losing Super Bowl XXXII.

The most exciting part of the whole Super Bowl XXXI experience came during a special gathering for the players, coaches, executives, and their wives in June, when I finally put a

Super Bowl ring on my finger. Nothing can ever take away the excitement of being a champion and finally fulfilling your dream.

That did something for me as athlete, but to be honest with you, it didn't do much for me as a person. It didn't change my life in any way, good or bad. And maybe that sounds strange or ungrateful, but I think it goes right back to what Solomon taught us in Ecclesiastes and John told us in 1 John: fulfillment is not found in worldly things but in godly things.

Achieving my goal made me realize even more that there are a lot more important things outside of football. There's a championship in life that I'm trying to win. That championship is to try to have as much impact as possible on people's lives. If we win another Super Bowl, we'll have a great celebration. But I'd hate to know some of my teammates died without being with God. Putting a ring on my finger wouldn't make up for a guy going to hell. I'll show off my ring, but I can't take it with me. If I can have an impact on lives, that's my main goal in life.

LOVE GOD AND YOUR NEIGHBORS

Jesus answered him, "The first of all the commandments is:
'Hear, O Israel, the LORD our God, the LORD is one. And
you shall love the LORD your God with all your heart, with
all your soul, with all your mind, and with all your
strength.' This is the first commandment. And the second,
like it, is this: 'You shall love your neighbor as yourself.'
There is no other commandment greater than these."

Mark 12:29–31 NKJV

Sean Jones, one of my former Green Bay teammates, still recounts the advice his grandfather gave him years ago.

"Son," his grandfather said, "always remember this: your marriage will never be successful unless you die married. Some people are married for twenty, thirty, even forty years, then get a divorce. That's not a successful marriage. A successful marriage is when you die married."

Sean's granddad was a wise man, and I think the advice holds true for a successful life too. To have a successful life, you have to love God while you live and when you die.

The Bible says he who endures to the end shall be saved (Matt. 10:22). David says in Psalms that he proclaims God's salvation daily (96:2). I understand my life is a daily process. Every time God delivers me from something, it teaches me a lesson or builds my character, and to me, that is salvation, because it's drawing me closer to God.

My concept of receiving Christ is different from some people's concept. I think it's a heart change, not just a mouth change. Romans 10:9 says that if we confess with our mouths that Jesus is Lord and believe in our hearts that God has raised Him from the dead, we shall be saved.

Some people sit there and say, "Okay, I believe in Jesus. I confess with my mouth." But the thing is, their hearts haven't changed. And we need to have a change of heart before we can experience God's love.

Let me give you an example from Scripture to show what I mean about having a change of heart. According to Luke 10, an expert of the law approached Jesus and asked Him what he must he do to have eternal life. Jesus asked him a simple question: what does the law say? And the lawyer answered with the Old Testament answers: "You shall love the LORD your God with all your heart, with all your soul, with all your strength, and with all your mind," and "your neighbor as yourself" (v. 27 NKJV).

Jesus said the lawyer had answered correctly, and if he followed that advice, he would inherit eternal life. But—typical lawyer—the man asked somewhat sarcastically, "Who is my neighbor?"

And Jesus responded with the parable of the Good Samaritan. You probably know the story. A man was robbed, stripped of his clothes, beaten half to death, but a priest and a Levite walked right by and didn't stop to help him. Yet a Samaritan stopped and bandaged his wounds, put the man on his own donkey, took him to an inn, and paid the innkeeper to look after him. Now, you have to remember, Jews despised Samaritans, looked down upon them as half-breeds in race and in spirit. But what Jesus was telling this man is that until you learn to love those people you despise, that until you have a heart change, you will not inherit eternal life.

The lesson about racism is just as important today as it was two thousand years ago. Because abolition is less than 150 years old and the civil rights movement is less than forty years old, I think our race problems are more serious than they were in Jesus' time.

Only if we put our differences aside and love our neighbors as ourselves can we love God too. Because loving your fellow man is a prerequisite of loving God. The Bible tells us so in 1 John 4:20: "If someone says, 'I love God,' and hates his brother, he is a liar; for he who does not love his brother whom he has seen, how can he love God whom he has not seen?" (NKJV).

SHARE YOUR FAITH

Go into all the world and preach the gospel to every
creature. He who believes and is baptized will be
saved; but he who does not believe will be condemned.
And these signs will follow those who believe:
In My name they will cast out demons; they will
speak with new tongues; they will take up serpents;
and if they drink anything deadly, it will by no
means hurt them; they will lay hands on
the sick, and they will recover.

Mark 16:15–18 NKJV

I've won a Super Bowl. I've gone to more consecutive Pro
Bowls than anyone in NFL history. I've collected more sacks
than anyone. I've made the NFL's All-Time Team. I've spread
my wealth and I've spread my faith. I've been saved and I've led
others to the Lord. God has blessed me with miracles and
helped me perform miracles.

But the most exciting thing in my life was my trip to Israel.
Sara and I were the celebrity hosts of a 317-person group that
toured historic Christian sites for nine days in March 1998.

I've been a Christian for a long time, but I've never had an
experience like it. My whole purpose in going to Israel was not to
go on tour or vacation, but to have a life-changing experience,

and we did. I'm challenged even more now to seek God and understand His purpose for my life. Because I realize it's much bigger than football.

These biblical sites were just ancient, foreign names in black and white before. Seeing them in person made the Bible come alive for me. The land is nothing but rock, and anything the Israelites built, they had to dig through rock. I saw city built on top of city, everything built out of rock, and I'm not talking about little rocks, I'm talking about huge rocks, boulders. It made me wonder how they could move them and lift them thousands of years ago.

I saw a water tunnel where they dug 140 feet through rock with a hammer and chisel. I joked that one piece of rock looked like a baby crib, and the tour guide said, "It was." I was totally impressed with how they made their cities and homes and even their furnishings out of rock and stone, and I thought how lazy and spoiled we are in America.

I saw all the places Jesus walked—from Tiberias to Capernaum to Jerusalem—to minister to the people. He didn't walk straight-and-narrow streets; He walked up and down mountains. Not hills. Mountains I couldn't even climb. Just to pray. That challenged me. I'm convinced even more that Jesus was no weak chump. They say a carpenter was a wood cutter, but shucks, I think Jesus was probably a rock cutter too. Jesus did some hard work, and it made me realize I can't complain about petty stuff or take anything for granted.

The trip also gave me a chance to preach and reach a lot of people. Many came just to meet Sara and me, but I assure you they left with something much more. It was a once-in-a-lifetime experience for them—and for Sara and the kids and me.

One lady in her sixties or early seventies told me that she'd actually come to Israel to shake my hand so she could go home and die. She had given up on her life.

But she told me, "Since I've been here and seen the way you

and Sara minister, you've made me realize that not only do I want to live, but that God has something for me. My husband and I have been married fifty-one years, and for the first time in all those years, I saw him cry when you spoke."

We were visiting the garden tombs when another lady in her sixties told me, "I came here just to meet you and give you a message, but I'm not going to give it to you because I know you're getting tired of being used—and because this experience has really challenged me and made me realize that I have something to live for."

And I said, "First of all, you don't have to apologize. And second, I was the attraction for you to come, but you're leaving here with a lot more than Reggie White. You're leaving here with a God-given experience."

Even though most of those people were older, I told Sara, "Man, I feel like we're their mother and father." We received testimony after testimony from people letting us know how much they appreciated it, how much the trip changed their life.

But you know what? Our lives were changed even more than theirs were.

LEAVE A LEGACY

I have fought the good fight, I have finished the race, I have
kept the faith. Now there is in store for me the
crown of righteousness.
2 Timothy 4:7–8 NIV

The most moving site on our tour of Israel was the garden
tomb where it is believed Jesus rose from the dead. Obviously,
we couldn't feel the pain of His crucifixion. But we could gain
some sense of it, and we could share the joy of His resurrection.

The Romans crucified only the most despicable criminals,
and it was a macabre way to die. Our tour guides showed us
how the Romans drove heavy, wrought-iron nails through the
victims' wrists, then turned their feet sideways and nailed
through their ankles. The victims would have to pull themselves
up to keep their heads up, because when they lost energy and
their heads fell down, their lungs collapsed, and they died
through suffocation. It usually took three or four days to die,
but Jesus died quicker because He gave up the ghost.

Jesus was crucified for no reason at all. An innocent man
died on the cross for me and you and everybody in this world.
He's a great example of what true leadership and true commitment are.

Another example can be found in the Old Testament and

Daniel 3, when Shadrach, Meshach, and Abednego refused to worship King Nebuchadnezzar's ninety-foot image of gold even when the king ordered them thrown into a blazing furnace. They told the king that God would deliver them if they were thrown in the fire. They said so based not on certainty but on faith in God. The Lord spared them, and the king was so impressed, he promoted them and praised God.

They were willing to die for what they believed in. Most of the men committed to God in the Scriptures were willing to die for Him.

We had people in this country who would die for a cause up until the sixties. But I wonder how many would die for a cause today. I wonder how many are willing to die for Jesus.

I know I wasn't willing in the early eighties. I was afraid to take my ministry to streets filled with violence and drugs in the toughest parts of Philadelphia. But then the Lord reminded me of Revelation 12, when Michael and the angels fought the great dragon called Satan and hurled him out of heaven and back to earth (vv. 7–9). And I was reminded of a quote by the great civil rights leader, Dr. Martin Luther King Jr.: "If you can't find a cause to die for, you've got nothing to live for."

And so, beginning in 1989, I took my message to the oppressed, because they're the ones who need it the most. I decided I would stand up for the poor, for my family, for Jesus Christ, and I was willing to die for God and the people I'm trying to reach on His behalf. My wife is willing to sacrifice herself and her husband too. We've chosen that path because we've seen people's pain.

Before I die, I want to make a difference. And when I'm laid to rest, I want my family and friends, my coworkers and community, to revel in my accomplishments. So now, while I can, I want to create a legacy to be proud of.

People cheer for me because I'm a football player. I want people to cheer because I impact lives. Playing football, sacking quarterbacks, knocking guys out—that can't change anybody's life. But because football gives me celebrity status, I can change lives through my ministry, and that's much more important than football.

Winning the Super Bowl was a blessing God gave me for all the work I've put in, so it was exciting as an athlete, but as a person, I know there's much more. There's another championship I want to win, and that's to change people's lives by spreading the good news of God.

Celebrities are the most overrated people in the world. We put them on pedestals where they don't belong. The only one who belongs on a pedestal is God. But since America does look up to athletes, I want to be a positive role model and show people how the Bible can provide answers to all their problems.

Maybe after I retire at the end of this season, the media won't stick a microphone in my face every day and people won't look up to me as much. I've heard ministers and other people call ex-players has-beens, and maybe I'll be considered a has-been too. If people don't want to listen to me because I don't play football anymore, then that's fine.

But I believe God has much bigger plans for me—something that will have much greater impact than football, that will be much bigger than maybe I ever imagined. I want to be involved in full-time ministry. I want God to use us to enter people's lives more in deed than in word.

I know what I want to do.

I know what God is calling us to do.

I know if a Super Bowl ring is all I ever achieve, I will have failed. And I don't plan to fail.

I plan to leave a legacy.

ABOUT THE AUTHORS

Green Bay defensive end Reggie White is an ordained minister, a twelve-year veteran of the NFL, a Super Bowl champion, a twelve-year Pro Bowl starter, and future Hall of Famer. He also received the 1997 WOW award for Christian Sports Figure of the Year. He and his wife, Sara, have founded many inner-city ministries. They and their two children split their time between homes in Wisconsin and Tennessee. He is the author of *In the Trenches: An Autobiography.*

Steve Hubbard is a contributor to several magazines and the author of seven books including *Faith in Sports: Athletes and Their Religion on and off the Field.*